Nothing's Too Small to Make a Difference

Simple Things You Can Do
to Change Your Life & the World
Around You

Nothing's Too Small to Make a Difference

Simple Things You Can Do to Change Your Life & the World Around You

BY

WANDA URBANSKA AND FRANK LEVERING

JOHN F. BLAIR, PUBLISHER
WINSTON-SALEM, NORTH CAROLINA

The paper in this book meets the guidelines
for permanence and durability of the Committee on
Production Guidelines for Book Longevity
of the Council on Library Resources

Cover photograph — Martin Tucker
Photo stylist — Anne Waters
Jacket design — Debra Long Hampton

Library of Congress Cataloging-in-Publication Data
Urbanska, Wanda, 1956-
Nothing's too small to make a difference / by Wanda Urbanska and Frank
Levering ; foreword by Ed Begley, Jr.
     p.   cm.
ISBN 0-89587-297-8 (alk. paper)
1. Simplicity. 2. Conduct of life. I. Levering, Frank. II. Title.
BJ1496.U73 2004
646.7—dc22
2004009345
Printed in Canada

To our son, Henry Urbanski Levering,
and to our future: Young people everywhere

Contents

Foreword

When Wanda Urbanska, Frank Levering, and their six-year-old son, Henry, arrived in my Studio City home one February morning earlier this year, I was meeting strangers who lived a long way from Southern California. Though I'd heard of their work, our paths as advocates of treading lightly on our environmentally fragile planet had never crossed. But the two families didn't remain strangers for long. While Henry played with my four-year-old daughter, Hayden, I got acquainted with Wanda and Frank, comparing notes and working all morning with a television crew on their much-needed series for public television, *Simple Living with Wanda Urbanska.*

That time together launched a friendship. Beyond that, it reminded us why we three adults—along with my wife, Rachelle—work as we do to heighten awareness about environmental stewardship. As Hayden and Henry explored various corners of our house and yard, the answer was always in earshot: *those children.* We do the work we do as environmental activists because children around the planet will come of age in the world we pass on to them.

For quite a few years now—since I first glimpsed those stirring photographs of a rising earth taken from the moon—I've tried in a variety of ways to underscore the idea that one person's actions can make a positive difference for our environment. Individuals play a vital role in the health of our planet's overall ecosystem, and there are many things all of us can do to make our common home a better place to live. In choices I and many others have made involving home energy use, food, waste, and transportation, I've learned that—as Wanda and Frank say—"nothing is too small to make a difference," that any positive step, large or small, is helpful. It's important to remember, I've learned, that among those thousands of things each of us can do, you don't have to do all of them. Anything helps! Not everyone can change the entire world, but we can all try our hardest to change our little piece of it.

From many years of committed activism, I know that getting involved in organizations that work to help solve our environmental crisis—that work through political, business, and community channels—is an important piece of the puzzle. But I also know that taking action in your daily way of living is both crucial for the big picture that confronts us all and deeply rewarding on a personal level.

That's why Wanda and Frank's book is "must reading." If you are looking for down-to-earth, levelheaded ideas to live your life in a simpler, more thoughtful, more environmentally responsible way, *Nothing's Too Small to Make a Difference* is the book to read. If you are looking for inspiration to live your life in closer alignment with your values, *Nothing's Too Small to Make a Difference*—with its delightful stories and useful tips—is the book for you. Here's a book that could not be timelier, both for you and for our planet.

As they do in their television series and in a previous book, *Simple Living: One Couple's Search for a Better Life*, Wanda and Frank tell stories of transformation wonderfully well. And they gently connect with an American public eager for change, yet still searching for practical solutions. Our world makes progress thanks to the practical idealism of people like Wanda and Frank. For many years now, they have been living lives that speak to our better natures, that spur us to action. *Nothing's Too Small to Make a Difference* is the distillation of years of life-tested wisdom, of hands-on experience in living life more consciously. Read this book and new possibilities will blossom in you—like the blossoms on the cherry trees in Frank and Wanda's orchard in the Blue Ridge Mountains of Virginia.

Someday soon, I hope to bring my family to visit that beautiful orchard that I have only read about. In the meantime, there is this important book for all of us. Read this life-changing guide to the best that's deep within you, and your own life, surely, will make a greater difference.

Ed Begley, Jr.
Studio City, California
April 2004

Acknowledgments

A book comes into being by a mysterious alchemy otherwise known as blood, sweat, and tears. But that's only half of it. The other half of the story of *Nothing's Too Small to Make a Difference* is the human circle of encouragement and support surrounding the two authors. That human circle has made all the difference for us, and it is too big a circle for us to acknowledge here every person in it. But we can at least thank some of the people to whom we are indebted, fellow travelers who believe as we do that small steps lead to big steps—that, down the road, small is big.

This book is a book and not merely a gleam in the authors' eyes thanks to the pragmatic visionaries at John F. Blair, Publisher, themselves the heirs to the vision of the brilliant and idiosyncratic company founder, John F. Blair, in publishing singular and culturally stimulating works. From the outset, we felt wonderfully supported by the hardworking folks at John F. Blair. We also felt a rare sense of kinship with them as fellow businesspeople and practical idealists who are deeply involved in the life of our communities. We thank Carolyn Sakowski, the delightfully modest president of John F. Blair, for her early and sustained faith in us and our work. We also thank the tireless (and charming!) Anne Waters, Ed Southern, Sue Clark, Debra Long Hampton, and Kim Byerly, each of whom we have gotten to know and admire. To Steve Kirk, editor in chief, who pored over the manuscript and offered numerous and incisive editorial suggestions, we are indebted for as bracing and fine a line-edit as two authors could hope for anywhere.

A number of people helped "birth" the book, offering suggestions for subject matter and for persons to talk to, offering their moral support, and, in some cases, offering their guest rooms in our travels! We particularly want to thank old friends Carol Holst and Mal and Ellen Hoffs in Los Angeles and Alex Kern and Becca

Grunko in Boston for their warm hospitality as we went about our work. On the home front, Pat Gwyn Woltz provided the sort of day-to-day moral support that could only come from a true guardian angel. And Pat's daughter, Mary Woltz, contributed important ideas to our "idea bank." Ann Vaughn, our dear friend in Mount Airy, looked for—and found—every opportunity to help, often at great personal sacrifice. Also on the home front, key players in our North Carolina circle of support were Copey Hanes, Zach Smith, and Nick and Nancy Bragg of Winston-Salem; Ann Belk of Charlotte; and Paul and Cecelia Belk, Hattie Brintle, David Bradley, Swanson Snow, Rich Kunkel Gene Rees, and Burke Robertson of Mount Airy. A special thanks goes to Linda Brinson of Stokes County, North Carolina; Dr. Aldona Wos of Greensboro, North Carolina; and Lady Blanka Rosenstiel of Charlottesville, Virginia. Our talented office manager and editorial assistant, Laura Lyerly, contributed mightily to every phase of the book's development. Without all these folks, both the book and its companion public-television series, *Simple Living with Wanda Urbanska*, would be much the poorer.

To the National Board of Advisers for our public-television series, we owe a special debt for their early faith in the importance of the ideas in the series and in the book, as well as for their continued encouragement. In addition to Paul Belk, Nick Bragg, Carol Holst, Burke Robertson, Ann Vaughn, and Pat Gwyn Woltz, the board members include Cecile Andrews, Max Carter, Linda Fuller, Judith Helfand, Melvin Johnson, Stan King, Frances Moore Lappé, Dale Pollock, Jane Preyer, Lisa Renstrom, Juliet Schor, Michelle Singletary, Anne Slepian, Sarah Susanka, Kathy Treanor, John E. Wear, Jr., and Craven Williams. To each of them—leaders and public servants—thank you.

Invaluable to this book was the support of the Worldwatch Institute in Washington, D.C., particularly that of director of research Gary Gardner and staff researcher Erik Assadourian, who in addition to his help with the book was instrumental in Worldwatch's sponsorship of our television series at the D.C. Environmental Film Festival. Gary and Erik and their critical, internationally acclaimed work at Worldwatch have been a tremendous inspiration to us.

We would also like to give special thanks to Dr. Melvin Johnson, advisory board member for the television series and provost and vice chancellor of academic affairs at Winston-Salem State University, and Dr. Harold Martin, chancellor at Winston-Salem State, for their friendship, encouragement, and continuing reminder of the importance of public education. Harold and Mel were guiding lights for us, as was Dale Pollock, dean of filmmaking at the North Carolina School of the Arts and an early and ardent supporter.

For their help, we would like to thank the Reverend Fletcher Harper, president of Partners for Environmental Quality, along with Dick Hanratty and Alan and Connie Foster.

This roster of acknowledgments cannot be complete without invoking the names of longstanding supporters who, once again, joined hands in a wide circle of encouragement. We wish to thank our agent, Charlotte Sheedy, for her trenchant wisdom and boundless generosity; friends Linda Fuller (cofounder of Habitat for Humanity), Liz Brody, and Bonni Brodnick, for doing what friends do best—listen to us talk; and family members Marie U. Whittaker, Jane U. Robbins, Margaret and Sid Raley, Ruth Kelley, Ralph and Patty Levering, Elizabeth and Lou Lindsey, Montague Kern, Jane Ballus, Betty Blackburn, and Dan and Mary Smith, for seeing both the book and the television series as harbingers of hope, both for our families and for our nation and world.

We would be remiss if we did not acknowledge the fine folks at Smead Manufacturing Company in Hastings, Minnesota—especially Sharon Avent, Al Arends, and Michelle L. Hanson. They represent the leadership in a visionary company—people who recognize the importance of the concepts presented in this book—both to the business world and to humanity itself. For their sponsorship of the first run of the Simple Living television series, we express our deepest appreciation.

Finally, we want to thank Henry Urbanski Levering, our son. As we worked on this book, Henry spent many an hour in our office reading and playing, with every bit as much patience and good humor as most adults possess, ourselves included. Henry and his peers inherit the world we adults now create. Our fondest wish is that Henry will have good reason to thank us.

Introduction

Are you looking for a more meaningful, less frenetic life? Do you want your life to contain less and matter more? Would you like to make day-to-day choices that will help ensure a rosier future for yourself, your children, and the world itself?

If your answer to any of these questions is *yes*, then this book is for you.

America is a great nation because we believe in great things: the democratic process; human equality; life, liberty, and the pursuit of happiness. At our best, we rise to the greatness of our beliefs, and we fervently want the best of our ideals to extend into the future—for the nation and the world that our children will inherit, the world that we hope our son, Henry, now six, will live to see.

And yet we are in trouble—big trouble. While real or perceived threats from abroad continue to preoccupy us, too many of us are concerned in the macro sense about environmental crises and in the micro sense about the erosion of the quality of our lives. Too many of us are time stressed, exhausted, disconnected from each other and from community life. We hurry through life stewing over the injustices of yesterday, worrying about the calamities of tomorrow, failing to be present in the here and now. And all too often, we're not even likely to remember the conversation we had with a friend over lunch thirty minutes ago because we're too preoccupied with what's next on our personal to-do list.

Big Media, with its advertisements for our consumer culture, shadows us wherever its airwaves, sound bites, and billboard messages meet our ears and eyes, which these days is almost everywhere—in supermarkets, in our vehicles, at the workplace, on our computer screens, at airports, in bus terminals, and even in the once commercial-free zones of schools and universities.

Too many of us are consuming recklessly, drowning in *stuff*, and leading rat-race lives. Too many of us have a nightmarish sense of impending environmental doom yet believe there is nothing we as individuals can do. The demands on us are just too overwhelming. We're not responsible for this environmental mess, nor are we able to do a thing to dig ourselves out.

We used to feel that way. Our lives in Los Angeles in the 1980s often gave us that feeling of paralysis. In a huge city choked with cars and smog, what could we as two hardworking young adults do to improve the quality of the air or water? In our fast-lane careers in journalism and film, what could we do to feel less stressed, more connected to each other and the community, less worried about keeping up with the Joneses? Overwhelmed by these seemingly insurmountable problems, we did little.

All that changed in 1986 when we moved to an orchard in Virginia's Blue Ridge Mountains just north of Mount Airy, North Carolina, and streamlined and redirected our lives. This book is here to tell you that the problems are *not* too big and that one person is *never* too small. *Nothing's Too Small to Make a Difference* challenges the self-defeating assumption that one person—and one action—can't make a difference. It's a book written by Americans for Americans. And by that, we mean simply this: We Americans are a can-do people. If something's broken, we fix it. We are, and have been since our nation was founded, a people who put our great ideals to the test of practicality.

Nothing's Too Small to Make a Difference does exactly that. It's written not by dreamers—though we are proud to dream of a better world—but by patriotic, practical, hands-on businesspeople and parents, two people in midlife who've seen a lot of the world and how it works. *Money* is not a dirty word to us. Running a business and making a profit are two things we've learned how to do. Possessions— if valued but not worshiped—can be meaningful life companions. We share many, perhaps most, of the challenges you face, and we speak your language. Our son's world and the world of your children and grandchildren are one and the same.

The suggestions this book offers are both proven and practical. In eight chapters, four written by each of us—chapters dealing with time, money, work, the environment, children and the young, community life, health and food, and spiritual growth—*Nothing's Too Small to Make a Difference* gives you tools that have worked for us and others and can work for you. Our book diagnoses the problems and never underestimates their magnitude, yet gives you practical ways to solve them.

Our goal is to empower you to make changes in your life by taking baby steps, then larger strides, and to connect the dots between where you are now and where you can go to make a difference.

This book is meant as a companion volume for our television series—*Simple Living with Wanda Urbanska*—as well as an advice book that stands on its own merits. In the series, some of the stories we share in these pages are told more visually, with an eye for visual impact. Yet the mantra for the book and the series is the same: *Nothing's too small to make a difference.*

As in two of our earlier books, *Simple Living* and *Moving to a Small Town*, what has inspired us most is learning the personal stories of the many, many people for whom nothing is too small. Real people who live in the real world demonstrate the truth of this every day. In this book, we invite you to be inspired by the lives, stories, and suggestions of the many people who have inspired us.

As with our 1992 book, *Simple Living*, we continue to notice that when you try to simplify your life, certain themes recur. Lifestyle simplification invariably cycles back to stewardship of your time, your money, and the environment. It involves making thoughtful choices about what you buy and consume and how you relate to others—the significant others in your life and the less central people who come into and go out of your life but who make an impact.

Readers should know that the changes they make can have multiple and overlapping benefits. For instance, if you decide to take public transportation instead of driving your car to work—even only one day a week—this change will save you money, help the environment, build community, and make you a thoughtful steward of time and resources. You'll note that the same ideas for solving problems and managing resources crop up in multiple chapters in our book. For instance, if you're looking for ways to find more time, one of our many suggestions is to consider reducing your television consumption; if you're looking to build community or improve your family life or health, we once again suggest revisiting your relationship with television. We repeat central tips consciously in order to reinforce the message of simplicity, which is after all about interconnectedness, about bringing the various parts of our lives together.

Many of the tips contained in this book are meant as starting points for bringing simplicity into your life through nothing's-too-small choices. We have never wanted to devise a ten-point plan, but rather to offer up what has worked for us and others in the hope that it will inspire you to make changes, as it has us. As our friend Carol Holst told us, advice is great, as far as it goes. But what's really exciting is the moment when you start to make your own connections, find your own choices, and begin the journey to real freedom.

Wanda Urbanska and Frank Levering
Mount Airy, North Carolina
March 2004

Nothing's Too Small
to Make a Difference

Simple Things You Can Do
to Change Your Life & the World
Around You

CHAPTER 1
Time

*"Since World War II . . . we as a society have chosen
money over time, and this unconscious value pattern has
had a powerful and less-than-beneficial impact on the
quality of our collective lives."*
—John de Graaf, editor, *Take Back Your Time*

How often do you feel pressed for time? If your answer is "rarely," you are an exception. Time scarcity is the defining reality for most Americans today, whether we be two-career couples, single parents, single people, homemakers, men or women of every age group and occupation—or even children. We run on a treadmill, in many cases so time-starved that we'll cut someone off on the freeway if he threatens to swipe a few seconds from our precious reserve, or step on someone's sentence before she has a chance to complete it, or walk out of a meeting, a class, or even a church service if our attention starts to flag. There's always something else to do, some other, more pressing claim on our time. And so we rush through our minutes, our days—our lives—never quite taking hold of ourselves or the experience that we're supposed to be living.

"Timelock," writes Ralph Keyes in his 1991 book of the same title, is the "condition that occurs when claims on our time have grown so demanding that we feel it's impossible to wring one more second out of a crowded calendar." The old expression "There aren't enough *hours* in a day" is now "There aren't enough *minutes* in an hour" or even "There aren't enough *seconds* in a minute." Clearly, we're all victims of the acceleration syndrome, in which time moves faster and faster. But it's hard to tell which came first. Are we living fast because life is accelerated, or is life accelerated because we've all stepped up the pace? Or are the two factors combined fueling the frenzy?

The accelerated pace of our lives—along with the lack of what Wisconsin physician and author Richard A. Swenson calls "margin"—has become an accepted fact of modern life. Margin is a mental, physical, and emotional condition that is the opposite of overload; it is that cushion of time that allows us to maneuver gracefully through our lives; it is the reserve of energy, emotion, and time held for unanticipated situations and crises. But only recently have medical and mental-health professionals begun to examine the physical and psychological implications of our time-starved, marginless existence—as well as to point to solutions.

"The U.S. is not very healthy compared to other industrial countries, despite spending almost half of the world's health-care budget," writes Dr. Stephen Bezruchka, a physician and professor at the University of Washington's School of Public Health, in the 2003 *Take Back Your Time* handbook. "If we don't have time to form friendships and be seriously involved in organizations and our political process, our health will suffer. This . . . is well established in the literature of public health."

So why are we so time strapped? "Working too much," Bezruchka writes, "leaves us little time for other important aspects of our lives."

Why the Time Crunch?

Little more than a generation ago, social scientists predicted that technological advances would usher in a golden era of leisure in which we'd all have gobs of time for self-development, social betterment, and pleasure seeking. But in fact, Americans have never been more work centered.

Today's employees face increasingly heavy work loads. More is expected of each of us; in many fields, one worker is asked to do the job two or three had performed in the past. Statistics show that we are working ever-longer hours. According to Boston College sociologist Dr. Juliet Schor, from 1973 to 2000, the average American worker added "an additional 199 hours to his or her annual schedule"—or nearly five new forty-hour work weeks per year. Indeed, Schor, author of *The Overworked American*, calls the United States the world's "standout workaholic nation," now surpassing even that longtime workaholic giant, Japan.

What's more, the number of hours we spend on the job doesn't tell the whole story. If we're professionals, we're expected to keep up with our field, with the overload of information coming at us from multiple sources and directions. Add to that community service, company service, higher and continuing education, and networking to keep other job prospects alive—a vital activity in this era of downsizing and layoffs—and we're looking at a whole host of work-related demands on our time that further shrivel the sliver of time left over for us.

Possession Overload

With the advent of the McMansion syndrome—as housing size has skyrocketed in this country—we're responsible for larger personal spaces, which we tend to fill with more possessions, all of which translates into more to clean, maintain, store, and keep track of. We have more phone lines, more vehicles, more garages, more gadgets, and more storage space—along with a mind-boggling number of options and choices—than any people before us. To cope with so much on our plates, in our closets, and on our minds, multitasking has become a way of life. We chat on our cell phones while chugging java, chopping onions, listening to the radio, and jotting to-do lists.

Getting Your Time in Balance

Time is the oft-neglected stepsister that gets lost in the shuffle when we think about the big life issues of work, love, happiness, health, and money. And time is easy to slight because it's hard to see, hard to get your arms around. But if you do not learn to manage your time, you'll find that it will slip through your fingers. Once you do learn to work with time, to *go* with it—to spend it freely rather than hoard it—you will gain immense rewards in the form of life satisfaction. By knowing where your time is going and helping to direct that flow, you can make time your handmaiden, not your obstacle, as you advance toward your life's highest priorities.

Time: More Precious Than Money

I've devoted a great deal of my professional time in recent years to fund-raising for our public-television series on simple living. Before I embarked on the project, a number of people warned me against it, citing the thanklessness of the task.

You'll have to develop a thick skin, they said, because you'll face frequent rejection and discouraging projections.

Though there was truth in those admonitions, I have learned a number of life lessons from the experience, especially about the centrality of time in building relationships and trust. Fund-raising and project building, like anything else worthwhile, take time.

I must admit to one occurrence during this process that surprised me and drove home a central point in the simple-living equation. I met a prominent, successful businessman who decided to contribute five thousand dollars to the project. He called our office to tell me about the gift and at the same time beg off a meeting scheduled for the next day. "If I mail you the check, do I still have to meet with you?" he asked, his voice pleading.

In that instant, I realized that, to this generous and well-intentioned man, time was more precious than money. In the grand scheme of things, he probably had his priorities straight. And though less financially affluent people tend to believe that their problems will diminish once they are more prosperous, when it comes to a feeling of time affluence, that is *not* generally the case.

"Timelock"

In fact, while time pressure appears to afflict everyone up and down the socio-economic scale, a number of experts on the subject agree that, in general, the wealthy are even more time starved than their less affluent brethren. "There is a paradoxical connection between too much income and too little time," writes Ralph Keyes in *Timelock*. "Leaner living will force us to slow down, take stock and select more carefully: what we buy, how we live, the ways we choose to spend our time." Indeed, when you think about it, time conservation is one of the strongest arguments for moving toward a simpler life.

Although the wealthy have the means to buy services from others that at least theoretically should save them time—they don't have to wash their cars, for example, or polish their silver or do yard work—they also tend to be saddled with possessions, properties, assets, stocks and bonds, people to manage, appointments to juggle. It's not so much the fundamentals that take a toll on their time; it's the *excess*. And the *time* to take care of these superfluities is the one thing that cannot be purchased.

Time: A Hidden Factor in Good Health

There's no getting around the fact that health maintenance takes time. While many people stay in grueling, unsatisfying jobs to keep their health insurance, it's ironic that what they often overlook are the simple things they can do for their health—and their overall quality of life—that require *time* rather than money. For instance, when you eat healthfully, it takes more time to select, prepare, and consume than it does when you eat fast food or pop a frozen entrée into the microwave. Farmers and home gardeners persuasively argue that your body prefers the produce that comes out of your own field or garden. And that says nothing about the personal satisfaction found in having grown something yourself. Slow-food advocates maintain that eating a leisurely meal over the course of hours aids your digestion as well.

To build health and reduce stress, many physicians recommend not twenty minutes but a full *hour* a day of exercise. A good night's sleep also consumes time. And happy relationships—another major ingredient of good health—also take time to build and maintain. This applies not only to close family and friends but also to community bonds. Public-health research confirms a phenomenon known as the "Roseto Effect," which demonstrates that participating in a strong, vital community has a striking and demonstrably positive effect on one's health, even among those who lack material wealth. You can read more about this in chapter 6.

Toward "Time Affluence"

It *is* possible to break out of the time-frenzied mode in which we live, by employing nothing's-too-small-to-make-a-difference strategies that have been effective for Frank and me and for others we've observed, interviewed, and befriended. By using them, you can take back your time and make it work for you.

In this chapter, I will lay out a few key strategies—along with numerous tips—that will give you a sense of unhurriedness, abundance, even luxury about your time. Once you reframe your thinking about time, you will develop a better sense of yourself, strengthen your ties to your community, and improve your health and happiness. As you develop time affluence, this newfound sense of grace and ease will transform your life and rub off on those around you. It is important to state that the best and most authentic transformation about time will take place in the context of moving to a greater sense of simplicity in your life. And as with most significant changes, it will take *time*.

Tracking Your Time

A common theme of those who write about time—from the poets to the time managers—is that it is fleeting. That's true enough, as far as it goes. But if you wish to transform your use of time, you need to know exactly where it's going and how you're spending it. But how do you do it?

One of the most basic ways to accomplish this is by doing a simple exercise we call "the Time Tracker." All you need is a notebook and a pencil and the determination to track exactly where you're spending your time for seven days. (Many of us are familiar with doing this sort of thing at work, as we record our appointments and projects, often in a calendar book.) The only real cost to you is your time. But much like the old saw that says it takes money to make money, it takes time to make time!

With this exercise, we ask you to note exactly how you spend your time during each waking hour for one week. For instance, start by noting the time you get out of bed. Record how long it takes to shower, dress, eat breakfast, exercise, get the kids ready for school, get to work, etc. Put it all down. Remember, nothing's too small to make a difference. If you spend two minutes every morning checking the tire pressure on the car, for instance, put that down. (Note: You do *not* have to track how you're spending your time at work, unless you elect to do a close analysis of your work situation.)

Tabulate Your Data: You May Be Surprised!

Be sure to keep your data faithfully for one full week. Do not let just one workday stand for the entire week, because you want to look for variations. After keeping this journal for a week, tabulate your data by adding up how many minutes or hours you spent on each activity.

For instance, for Francine Walden-Witherspoon, the weekday work commute added up to a hundred minutes, or one hour and forty minutes each day, including the ten-minute walk from her parking lot to work. That amounted to over eight hours per week. And this did *not* count the time spent squiring Christian to and from school. She hadn't realized that she spent so much time in the car. Until she consciously *tracked* her time, she assumed that she spent more time in the kitchen and more time cleaning house than she actually did. She was also chagrined to realize how little time she was spending with her son and at his school.

Nor did Francine realize that she spent two and a half hours per week on her *hair*. Though she'd always prized her thick, long red locks, she decided that it was time for a short bob that could be styled in less than ten minutes—preferably no more than five. Once she gave it some thought, she decided to put her time elsewhere. One other small thing she noticed once she turned the magnifying glass on herself was that she wasn't spending enough time with her daily newspaper to justify subscribing. All she ever did was scan the headlines, and that information

A Day in the Life of Francine Walden-Witherspoon

The daily log for Francine Walden-Witherspoon, a thirty-four-year-old single working mother with an eight-year-old son, reads like this:

6:00 A.M.—Wake up
6:00 A.M. to 6:05 A.M.—Stretch in bed; fight getting up
6:05 A.M. to 6:10 A.M.—Shower
6:10 A.M. to 6:15 A.M.—Make coffee; pop bread in toaster
6:15 A.M. to 6:25 A.M.—Eat breakfast; scan newspaper
6:25 A.M. to 6:30 A.M.—Dress
6:30 A.M. to 7:00 A.M.—Do hair
7:00 A.M. to 7:05 A.M.—Apply makeup
7:05 A.M. to 7:15 A.M.—Awaken Christian and help him get dressed
7:15 A.M. to 7:20 A.M.—Prepare Christian's lunch
7:20 A.M. to 7:40 A.M.—Drive Christian to school
7:40 A.M. to 8:20 A.M.—Drive to work
8:20 A.M. to 8:30 A.M.—Park and walk to work
8:30 A.M. to 5:00 P.M.—Work
5:00 P.M. to 5:15 P.M.—Chat with colleague who's going through a painful divorce; colleague drops me off at my parking lot
5:15 P.M. to 5:30 P.M.—Pick up dry cleaning, pizza for dinner
6:10 P.M.—Pick up Christian at after-school program (Note: pay late fee for arriving after 6:00 P.M.)
6:30 P.M. to 6:40 P.M.—Arrive home with Christian; unload car
6:40 P.M. to 6:45 P.M.—Unpack pizza; serve with pre-prepared salad and beverages
6:45 P.M. to 7:00 P.M.—Eat dinner while watching nightly news
7:00 P.M. to 7:10 P.M.—Clean up kitchen
7:10 P.M. to 8:00 P.M.—Work with Christian on homework
8:00 P.M. to 8:05 P.M.—Draw Christian's bath
8:05 P.M. to 8:20 P.M.—Put clothes in washer and fold pile of clothes
8:20 P.M. to 8:45 P.M.—Read *O* magazine
8:45 P.M. to 8:55 P.M.—Talk to sister-in-law and niece on phone
8:55 P.M. to 9:15 P.M.—Help Christian change into pajamas; read him book
9:15 P.M. to 9:30 P.M.—Browse through mail-order catalogs; place an order
9:30 P.M. to 9:45 P.M.—Peruse the personals
9:45 P.M. to 9:50 P.M.—Change toilet paper
9:50 P.M. to 10:00 P.M.—Remove makeup; cleanse face; brush teeth
10:00 P.M. to 10:30 P.M.—Watch TV
10:30 P.M.—Go to sleep

she could as easily get off the Internet, from radio headlines, or on TV. So she decided she'd either devote more time to reading the paper or cut back her subscription to Sunday-only service.

After you have followed this process yourself, make a list of your life priorities and ambitions, from small to grand. The desires can be as whimsical as "I want to build my amber jewelry collection" or as serious as "I'd like to pay off my college debt within three years" or "I'd like to save enough so that I can build a log home for my retirement." Your goals may be educational or aspirational: "I want to learn to speak Norwegian"; "I'd like to earn an advanced degree in business"; "I'd like to meet the love of my life."

Just as Francine did, after you tabulate where your time is going, look at the actual time spent on activities. Think creatively about how you can cut deadweight activities to find time for other pursuits. In Francine's case, she realized that her son would be young only once, and she wanted to spend more time with him. If she wanted to take time out of her commute, she needed to either move closer to her work or pursue a position closer to home. Since she was happier with her home than her job, she decided to send out her résumé. Luckily, in short order, she was able to find work just three miles from Christian's school. By taking a big-picture view of her life, she started saving nearly eight hours of time a week, most of which she reallocated into the "Christian" column.

Even if you don't make drastic changes like Francine did, the Time Tracker exercise offers a chance for self-reflection. It may reinforce what you really want to do. After completing this exercise, Sylvia Oberle, director of the Center for Community Safety at Winston-Salem (North Carolina) State University, found that she was bringing her work home at night and short-changing herself. She vowed to leave her work at the office, to say "no" more often to volunteer activities, and to find more time for herself. Justin Catanoso, executive editor of the *Business Journal* of Greensboro, North Carolina, decided that he needed to work "down time" into every day. With three school-age daughters and a wife at home, Justin could never conceive of completing his to-do list. Part of his challenge was to decide that "down time" is okay.

Mental Reframing

Once you've tracked where your time is going, placed that in the context of your overall life goals, and worked to make some adjustments, your next major challenge is to reframe the way that you think about time. For many people, making a paradigm shift from the standard time-crazed approach toward a more leisurely approach presents a daunting challenge. It's like trying to rethink a major given in our culture. As Richard Swenson writes in his book *Margin: Restoring Emotional, Physical, Financial, and Time Reserves to Overloaded Lives*, a marginless life is "cultural." Having margin in your life has become the exception to the rule—

what he calls "countercultural." But an ability to slow down the pace—if you can learn it—will pay dividends for years to come. Dividends to your peace of mind, your health, and your overall enjoyment of life.

How Do You Accomplish This?

Mental reframing involves coming to view time differently. Unlike money, which *can* be hoarded, you cannot literally hold onto your time. Time just goes. And no matter who we are or what we're worth, we all have exactly the same amount given to us every day. What we *can* do is control our feelings toward it.

If, for instance, you're stuck on the George Washington Bridge coming into New York City, as happened to Frank and me recently when we were driving to Boston for a television shoot, mental reframing allows you to go with this setback and not fight it. Obviously, no one likes being delayed. But if you end up both losing time and then beating up yourself and everyone around you because of this loss, you're twice defeated. You lose not only the time but also your peace of mind. Your blood pressure may soar. You may drive away your friends and antagonize your business contacts. So relax. Remind yourself that unexpected delays—unexpected demands on your time—were meant to be. Then see if you can salvage something from the experience. In our case, we turned on an NPR station and heard a rather disquieting call-in interview with an AIDS expert at the Centers for Disease Control, who warned that our national campaign against the deadly disease has been flagging. Because Frank and I were not budging an inch in traffic, we were able to devote our full attention to the program. That may be the single best part of any wait, unexpected or not: the ability to observe, to simply *be*.

The first thing to remember when you try to reframe your sense of time is not to attempt to control it. Time cannot be controlled, nor can its flow be stopped. All you can do is reframe your attitude toward it. Finally, relax. A relaxed frame of mind will help you accomplish your objectives more easily and organically.

Think about the way you feel when you've been happiest, and try to duplicate that state of mind. When you're working on a project you truly love and are committed to, you enter a timeless state in which you're not concerned about externals like how you look, how much is in your bank account, and whether your car needs an oil change. You are one with your mission. You are in what Mihaly Csikszentmihalyi calls "flow." It's like falling in love. No detail mentioned by the object of your desire is minor or intrusive. Everything is part of a wonderful, kaleidoscopic mosaic. Try to put yourself in that frame of mind about your time—especially when you're delayed. When you're in love, you aren't miserly with your time. It flows from you in your connection with the other person. Consciously apply these feelings to other times in your life. Slow down. Decelerate.

Live in the Present

A part of our difficulty with time is the barrage of information coming our way, which leads to a fragmenting not only of our thoughts and activities but of our sense of the present.

A North Carolina reporter who covers philanthropy once asked me what connection I saw between our time famine and the simplicity field. "Living in the present," I said without hesitation, "has become a thing of the past." This rare-for-me definitive retort made me wonder if the lack of time—for pleasure, for savoring our food and clipping our toenails, for chatting with friends on the street and reading our mail—is a driving force behind the national explosion of interest in simple living.

So the message for readers—for Americans—is to slow down and savor your time.

Fifteen Tips for Slowing Down

As you work on reframing your attitude, try taking some steps that will improve the quality of your time. If some of the following tips appeal to you, try them out.

1. Go without a watch

A few months ago, my watch strap broke. While I waited for a replacement to be sent, I went without a watch for an extended period. At first, I felt naked, stripped of something essential, as if a time device was hard-wired to my body. Then I opened my eyes and began noticing the multitude of time clues everywhere around me—on my computer, on the wall at the office, in the car, at banks on the street—and realized that I didn't really need a watch. Somehow, I found it liberating not to be strapped to time. As an exercise, try to go without your watch for a day or two and see if this connects you more organically to the ebb and flow of your personal time.

2. Prioritize, prioritize

One of the most efficient and organized Woman Wonders I know is Carol Holst, director of Seeds of Simplicity, a national membership organization based in Los Angeles that advocates simple living and provides members the educational tools to achieve it. Carol lives simply, which frees up her time for paid and volunteer work. I've often wondered how my dear friend manages to juggle all her different roles. "Right after simplify, simplify, simplify," she says, "it's prioritize, prioritize, prioritize." Once you develop your goals and the steps to reach them, she says, it's amazing how many decisions about time fall into place. She keeps "constantly shifting lists of to-dos." She willingly ditches less essential activities from the list as priorities change and she refocuses her goals.

3. Do it now

The old saying goes, "Every journey begins with the first step." So my advice is to get started, even if you're departing on a daunting journey. According to Carol Holst, the corollary to the old maxim *Carpe diem* ("Seize the day") is *Seize the time*. So if you want to do something—whether it's clean out your video collection or save for a trip to Australia—start now.

4. Pick your spots

Justin Catanoso, like myself an inveterate newspaper reader, has to read three papers for his work: the *Greensboro News and Record*, the *New York Times*, and the *Wall Street Journal*. One of his techniques is to write off sections of the world. "I know it sounds callous, but I just don't follow South America, for instance. So I don't read articles about that area. On the foreign front, I follow the Mideast closely." Allow yourself permission not to know something about everything. Freely admit to gaps in your knowledge. Follow closely your areas of interest.

5. Reflect on the big picture

Put in time every day to reflect on what's really important in your life: the big picture. For many people, writing in a journal is an effective way of documenting this. This is something I love to do, but if I don't have the time for lengthy passages and descriptions, I write down the best comment or moment of the day—or, if I want to remember it for some reason, the worst. It's important to note that these good thing are often something small—a moment or comment, like the prayer my six-year-old son, Henry, recently offered: "Please, God, let me live to old age so I can meet my grandchildren."

6. Turn off the TV and computer

Turn off the television on certain days, or limit its use to so many hours per day or so many shows. If you have a family, try to select common viewing experiences, which help to build bonds. Deal similarly with the computer and especially its Internet attractions.

7. Disconnect and reconnect

Unwire yourself. After a full workday, turn off your cell phone and your pager unless you're expecting an important call. The same goes for your land line. Turn on the answering machine and give your attention to the people you live with. Build a fire wall between your family or personal time and your work time. If you live alone, consider the hours spent with yourself nurturing your personal space and time to be "family" time.

8. Put your time into people

It takes time to build relationships. As John de Graaf writes in the preface to the *Take Back Your Time* handbook, "There's no present like the time." Take time to write letters and talk on the phone. Whenever you can, take what we call "face time"—that is, in-person time with the people you care about. Concentrate on really listening to them, deeply taking in what they are trying to tell you and what they are living through. Deep listening involves watching—no mental roving or multitasking. Don't be thinking about what you want to say next. Don't think about who else might be in the room. Just focus on what's on their mind.

9. Embrace "the healing power of doing good"

Every day, do something that has no direct benefit to you. It's what my friend, North Carolina author Peggy Payne, calls "the healing power of doing good." You'll find that your generosity will make you feel good about yourself, and that will pay unexpected dividends. One of those unexpected dividends will be a sense of free flow about time.

10. Stick with your decisions

Once you make a decision, stick with it. Think of how much time you spend changing and rearranging plans, considering and reconsidering options. Once you make a decision—once you make a lunch date or plan to take your child to *The Nutcracker*—do it. Even if you have to grit your teeth to get off that La-Z-Boy, even if you think you can't stick with your plan, just do it. Over time, this is a good habit to embrace, and it will end up saving you lots of time. If you don't employ this strategy, you'll find you're always on the lookout for an escape hatch—an exit strategy—from situations that threaten to siphon off your time. By adopting this practice, you'll weigh your decisions before you make them, not afterwards.

11. Allow yourself a cushion of time

In a time-pressed world, this strategy may seem counterintuitive, but I have developed a method that works whenever I employ it. Allowing yourself a cushion of time is a part of the mental reframing about time. If you're short on time, instead of trying to squeeze out every minute at work before leaving for your appointment, try instead to leave yourself a comfortable cushion of time. Figure how long it will take to get to your dental appointment, and leave fifteen minutes earlier than necessary. That way, you won't have to rush through a yellow light, and you won't get annoyed if someone nabs a parking space you thought had your name on it. It will allow you to arrive at the appointment before the designated time, calm, cool, and collected. Our friend Stan King of Santa Clara, California, employs this strategy, and has for a lifetime. It allows him to get where he needs to go unruffled. A corollary to this idea is to prepare yourself mentally for a wait. Then, if it doesn't occur, you'll be pleasantly surprised.

12. Inject pauses into every day

We used to call them breaks. Coffee breaks. Lunch breaks. My old office at the *Los Angeles Herald-Examiner* was equipped with cots where women could lie down and take naps in the day. What a great idea! If you can't go that far, at least get out of your chair and stretch for a few minutes several times a day. Get out on the street and walk around the building. Any pause out of your day will be helpful.

13. Stop multitasking

Whenever you can, stop multitasking. Focus all your energy on the chore at hand. I had this point brought home to me recently when I was trimming the ends of a bouquet of carnations Frank and Henry had brought me, while trying to visit with my son at the same time. You guessed it. The knife sliced my fingernail, cutting it down to the quick. "Don't try to do two things at once," Henry has reminded me several times since. Especially when one of them involves a knife.

14. Bundle your errands

When you go out for errands, spend your time more conscientiously by bundling them. It helps if you keep lists—on paper, on your palm pilot, or in your mind. That way, you'll waste neither time nor money.

"Take Back Your Time Day": The Movement

Frank and I have known John de Graaf for more than a decade. We first met him when the Seattle-based filmmaker included us in his documentary on—of all subjects—time. That documentary, which aired nationally as a PBS prime-time special in 1994, was called *Running Out of Time*. The subjects of time, environmental stewardship, and quality of life have all been part of de Graaf's life work. Therefore, it came as no surprise when he, along with a core group of members of the National Simplicity Forum and others, organized "Take Back Your Time Day" to focus national attention on the problem of overwork that is fraying our culture.

The first annual Take Back Your Time Day was held on October 24, 2003. The date was selected because it fell nine weeks before year's end. Those nine weeks were not accidental. They were the difference between the amount of time Americans work annually and what our European counterparts clock.

"We've allowed society to go out of balance in the direction of things we're obsessed with consuming at the expense of all other values," de Graaf told me over lunch at Seattle University at the 2003 Simplicity Forum Congress. We're losing personal time, civic participation, health, and connections with family, community, and nature for the sake of consumption, he said.

Time Day—which de Graaf, as the national organizer, envisions as an equivalent to Earth Day—could evolve into a national day of contemplation on which people take time to consider the quality of their lives, to achieve balance in their lives, and to discuss time and related issues. The goal is to make Time Day into a bipartisan issue. To that end, the Senate unanimously adopted a resolution that designated October as "National Work and Family Month." Numerous cities around the country—including Seattle and Mount Airy, North Carolina—issued proclamations designating Time Day as an official opportunity for Americans "to take part in activities and celebrations appropriate to the theme." As it evolves, Time Day will move toward a political agenda advocating for workers to win more vacation time, more flexible hours, and job sharing and other such options. "Unfortunately, we need legislation for much of this," said de Graaf. Once people "take back their time," they'll realize that, as de Graaf puts it, "there's no present like the time."

For more information on Time Day, visit www.timeday.org.

---

15. Keep your own house clean

Refuse to waste time dwelling on the faults of others. This means avoiding gossip and even the mental clutter of worrying about how other people fail you. Expect that other people will let you down, and be surprised if they do not. Put your time into constructive pursuits, figuring ways to save time and simplify your life. As my childhood friend Hallie Gay Bagley tells her son, Taylor, "Mind your own garden."

CHAPTER 2

Money and You

"Silence every motion proceeding from the love of money."

—John Woolman

"With the abolition of want and the fear of want, the admiration of riches would decay, and men would seek the respect and approbation of their fellows in other ways than by the acquisition and display of wealth."

—Henry George

"There is no wealth but life."

—John Ruskin

Money. When Wanda and I talk about money, it seems we often talk about our *relationship* with money. How we *feel* about money. What money's doing for us, and what we're doing for money.

What is *your* relationship with money?

"Relationship?" you say. "With *money?* Is this one of those touchy-feely, California kind of questions? Like, how do I get in touch with my Inner Dollar?"

Inner Dollar? Okay, since you brought it up, let's talk about that Inner Dollar and you.

Are you conflicted about money? On the one hand, do you pay attention to traditional spiritual wisdom and suspect that a love of money can come to no good? On the other hand, do you wolf down the latest bestseller on how to get rich (the best way to get rich, it's been said, is to tell others how to get rich) and pressure yourself or your spouse to make more money than you're earning now?

Do you and your Inner Dollar have a comfortable relationship? Or one that, for one reason or another, causes you more stress than a carload of in-laws banging on your door on Christmas Eve?

People can be downright strange about money. Not you, of course—about money, you're rational in every way! But some folks use money to control others. Either that or to feel superior because they're wealthy. Either that or to equate money with contentment. Money, it seems, can drive us like no other force on earth.

"We plunge ourselves into enormous debt and then take two or three jobs to stay afloat," observes author Richard J. Foster. "We uproot our families with unnecessary moves just so we can have a more prestigious house. We grasp and grab and never have enough."

John D. Rockefeller is said to have replied, when asked how much money he really needed, "Just a little bit more!"

Strange, isn't it? When all is said and done, money, many of us believe deep down in the Dungeon of Secret Thoughts (where the Inner Dollar lives), is the final measure of our worth.

The Ultimate Measuring Stick

But why shouldn't we regard money as the ultimate measuring stick? When Americans talk about money, our discourse invariably leads to the subject of wealth. Inescapably, it seems, we live in a culture that monetizes just about everything. And our consumer culture teaches us—in virtually every arena—that having more money and the things that money can buy will make us happier.

As Richard M. Ryan writes, "We have swallowed the idea that, to be well, one first has to be well off."

Happiness and money. Are they as inseparable as Abbott and Costello?

Other than latter-day hucksters in clerical garb, few sages have sanctified the connection. "Give me neither poverty nor riches," the author of Proverbs wrote. "A great fortune," wrote Seneca, the Roman philosopher who lived at the same time as Jesus, "is a great bondage." Jesus himself said, "You cannot serve God and mammon," mammon meaning riches or worldly gain, from the Aramaic word *mamona*.

Within the past decade, a number of researchers—including Tim Kasser at Knox College and Daniel Gilbert at Harvard—have scientifically verified these ancient spiritual truths.

In his book *The High Price of Materialism*, Kasser—an associate professor of psychology—draws on exhaustive studies of people with and without materialistic values to conclude that such values undermine well-being. He defines materialism as "the valuing of money, wealth, possessions, image, and status." "Lower well-being," he writes, "occurs because materialistic values are associated with poor satisfaction of psychological needs for security/safety, competence, belongingness, and autonomy/authenticity." In short, materialistic values lead to a greater risk of unhappiness in the form of anxiety, depression, low self-esteem, and problems with intimacy.

Beyond middle-class comforts, wealth makes little difference to your happiness, Daniel Gilbert's research concludes. Gilbert, a professor in Harvard's Department of Psychology, has studied "affective forecasting" in a wide variety of laboratory and field experiments. A burgeoning field in psychology, affective forecasting examines the ways in which we predict and act upon what will make us happy and unhappy—and how we feel afterwards about those predictions and actions.

Miswanting

Happiness, it turns out, is elusive. We may *predict* that a bigger salary or a fancier car will make us happy, but the outcome is that the happiness, the excitement about having that salary or car, wears off. What happens is that we *adapt*. Yet in making our affective forecasts, we tend to forget that we will adapt. Time and again, we're led by false expectations of pleasure to make choices that ultimately make us no happier, a process that Gilbert calls "miswanting."

"Every decision we make," Gilbert explained to Wanda and me recently, high in William James Hall on the Harvard campus, "is predicated on our belief that one course of action is going to make us happier than another. . . . So it's pretty common for people to be in love with a particular consumer good—say, a new car. They get the new car, and what happens? Well, for a little while, there's a lot of joy. Then that joy fades very quickly. What a person might conclude is, 'Gosh, things don't really bring me the happiness I thought.' But that is not what Americans conclude by and large because, as members of a consumer society, the conclusion is, 'It must not have been the right car. I probably need an even better one.' So that's how we get on this hedonic treadmill."

According to Gilbert, we've all heard that having a ton of money doesn't buy happiness. "The message is out there," he told us. "But the much stronger message that comes from the rest of our culture is that—of course—it does. You have to understand that people are trying to be as happy as possible. But societies, particularly consumer societies like ours, are not designed to make people as happy as possible. They are designed to make them consume as much as possible.

"Since people want happiness and societies want consumption, it is the job of society to convince people that consumption equals happiness. Otherwise, they are going to stop. So the message we are getting from every billboard, every magazine, every television show, every commercial is that more stuff equals more happiness. Pretty hard to resist that message when it is coming at you several hours per day from the time you are two years old."

Let the Joneses Keep Up with You

Pinpointing the psychological connection between money and happiness, then, can be the starting point for changing our relationship with money. It can help us understand what is *enough* in our lives. That piling on more money, more things, will never lead to Shangri-la. That unless we're truly materially impoverished, what we have now is just fine, thank you.

This is a simple idea, yet a hard one for many of us to embrace. Why? It's not only the daily bombardments Gilbert describes—the saturation advertising of our consumer culture. It's also the consumption habits of our reference groups—those damned Joneses who live next door. Who work where we work. Who *have* what *we* are entitled to have.

But are they happier than we are? Maybe they pretend to be. Maybe they even *appear* to be. But are they?

The reality is that, even as we gaze with envy at those infernal Joneses, many of us want to have our cake and eat it, too. We want the authentic life that comes with not trying to buy our way to happiness. But we also want what those Joneses have, leading to what Juliet Schor, in her book *The Overspent American*, calls "competitive consumption." It's difficult to resist when the Joneses have the latest SUV, when their kids have the latest Air Jordans. In the face of relentless peer pressure, becoming a *thoughtful* consumer can seem nigh on impossible.

But this is where the real work begins, because we can't have it both ways. It's the work not only of knowing what's really going on with the Joneses, but also of self-knowledge. It's the work of discovering what *you* enjoy, what *you* feel and think—what makes *you* unique. As you gain knowledge of yourself, you also fortify yourself against the old envy-and-spend cycle that kept you chasing the Joneses. Ultimately, you define your own style based on knowing who *you* are. True style, you discover, means simply being your own person.

A funny thing happens. No doubt, you've seen it among people you know.

When someone is his or her own person—self-determined and authentic, content with who he or she is—that person becomes magnetic. He or she *draws* people. Even the Joneses can't resist.

Unable to keep up with themselves—for who *are* they, really?—even the Joneses sense the presence, the magnetism, of authenticity and are pulled toward it almost against their will. It's the power of the *real* that draws them, a power unlike any other force on earth.

Infinitely stronger than the lure of money and possessions, self-knowledge—the possession of an authentic self—is what the Joneses would *kill* to keep up with. You have what everyone wants, what the great spiritual traditions have always known is the ultimate wealth of human existence.

Know the True Cost of Things

More than most of us, Henry David Thoreau valued his time. Not in the way that most of us do—by monetizing our time—but by analyzing true "life costs." "The cost of a thing," Thoreau said, "is the amount of what I call life which is required to be exchanged for it, immediately or in the long run."

In other words, because a thing—whatever it is—costs money, you trade a portion of your life for it. You trade your time. The true cost of that thing is something that is finite: your time, your life energy. Money, in essence, is a symbol of human energy. It represents a transfer of energy, an exchange of time expended.

Especially as we get older, this sobering truth about the real cost of anything we possess or work to possess can lead us to rethink our relationship with time. Aware as perhaps never before that each life is an hourglass, do we really want to sell our dwindling resource so readily? What is our time worth to us, particularly in light of what we now understand about happiness? Once we know ourselves, what do we want most—the things that money can buy, or the rest of our lives?

Get a Grip

All of which is not to say that money is unimportant when you simplify your life. It's certainly not to say that we can afford to be totally oblivious to the Almighty Dollar. In fact, the goal of achieving financial stability that's compatible with a simpler lifestyle forces us to pay closer attention to money than we have in the past. If anything, money becomes even more important, more valued, penny for penny. And not in a miserly sense, but in the spirit of American pragmatism, of Benjamin Franklin, of small-town and rural slow-lane common sense.

The point couldn't be more basic: Now that you know who you are and what you need, it's time to make smart—*very* smart—money decisions. Not get-rich smart, but smart for the big picture of your life. And when money's like a spoiled-brat kid—a tyrant in our lives who's running amok—we have to get a grip.

Concerned about our rising national debt during his time in office, Everett Dirksen, the late senator from Illinois, said, "A billion here and a billion there, and pretty soon you're talking real money."

Every year, more than a million Americans file for personal bankruptcy, their debts adding up to "real money." Millions more are in serious credit-card debt, up to their ears in stratospheric interest payments they can barely scrape together. Especially for those of us who are "financially challenged," who in one way or another don't want to face the reality of our spending habits, the simple icebreaker of tracking your spending is a great way to get real.

Become Your Own Financial Watchdog

There are numerous ways to become your own financial watchdog. The more elaborate methods will have you jumping through more hoops than a Barnum & Bailey lion. Don't bother. The idea here is twofold and simple. First, you'll need to shatter any illusions you may have about where you're actually spending your money. Second, you'll need to use your new grip on the facts to establish what *Washington Post* financial columnist Michelle Singletary calls "the two P's": priorities and a plan. That all-important plan, she told Wanda recently in her suburban Washington, D.C., home, is "an actual way of reaching those priorities."

Take a minimum of one month and jot down or enter into a computer file every expense you incur. That's right, every single one, no matter how small a drop in the bucket it may seem at the time, from a vending-machine Coke to a mortgage payment on your house.

Then, under any useful headings you choose, group those itemized expenses to see what the spending patterns are. With money, as Benjamin Franklin knew very well, nothing's too small to make a difference. *Nothing.* As you'll likely see, small things add up, just as tiny raindrops can soon become a flood.

Examining your spending under a financial microscope is not only a reality check. It creates mindfulness, the power of acute self-observation. Small things magnified under a microscope can raise large questions about what your priorities are.

For example, you may discover that though you *thought* planning for nine-year-old Susie's college education was a top priority, money you could be saving now is in fact being frittered away daily on pricey takeout coffee. Maybe that fancy coffee is truly indispensable, but are you at the same time getting the job done setting that money aside for Susie?

No mere exercise, tracking every expense forces you to start connecting the dots between priorities and actions.

Develop X-Ray Vision

Now that you know precisely where your money goes, and what you can and can't do about it as you develop an overall plan that reflects your priorities and values, the next step is to determine what you have at this moment. What are your total assets? Your total liabilities? What is your net worth? A bank would call this checkup a personal financial statement, the kind you need when applying for a loan. I'd call it a financial x-ray. It's a "Full Monty" self-exposure—no bone or organ hidden from view!

So why do that to yourself? Well, as you're sorting out your priorities and evolving an overall plan for your simpler life, you'll need to know exactly what resources are available for the things you want to accomplish. Odds are, it's been awhile since you've updated the information necessary to make accurate projections toward your emerging goals. Indeed, the results may surprise you. Better to be surprised now than later, when that unanticipated shortfall demands a midstream change of horses!

Budget, Budget, Budget

Complementing the x-ray and its companion plan is the procedure you're now equipped to do: draw up a budget. In the best of all worlds, a budget allows you to see every step ahead of you down your financial path—to see clearly where you can and can't go. Theoretically, at least, a budget provides for this sort of clarity because it matches actions with expenditures. If the money isn't there in your line-item budget, sorry, you don't suddenly quadruple the size of your kitchen. Period.

In practice, a budget, like all good monetary intentions, can fall prey to the temptations of deficit spending, just as it has of late on the local and state—as well as the federal—level. There's one pearl of wisdom—and one only—to keep in mind if you take your finances seriously enough to draw up a budget: Do not deviate! Once you do, it's a slippery slope to a thousand deviations, and then all is lost. Come hell or high water, don't budge from that budget!

This Bud(get's) for You!

Temporarily speaking, however, a budget should offer some flexibility. The granddaddy of all fiscally disciplined budgets is the *weekly* budget, which—particularly for credit-card prodigal sons and daughters—might just be the tonic you need. You allocate your money in weekly amounts and spend no more than the weekly allocation. If you need something that isn't covered in your weekly budget, you can save for it by spending under budget, rather than dip into savings. If at the end of the week you're in the black, then take a bow—and invest in the future by putting that surplus into savings.

Savings. As long as we're on the subject, it's worth noting that there's no better time to implement a savings plan than when drawing up your budget. "Pay yourself first," *Washington Post* columnist Michelle Singletary advises her readers. A regular savings payment can pay huge dividends over an extended period of time.

And don't cheat yourself. As Michelle recently told Wanda, "Now, many people hear that, and they swear that they will do it, but by the end of the week, they have borrowed from themselves."

Here's a fallback savings plan for those who just can't do it any other way. Credit this idea to get-rich guru Suze Orman, who is still otherwise locked in the mental prison of "money equals happiness." For daily purchases, spend paper money only. Put the change—all those coins—in a big jar. At the end of the month, transfer the contents of the jar—for most people, about forty to sixty dollars—into savings. *Voila!*—an instant savings plan.

More common than the weekly is the *monthly* budget. The longer unit of time perhaps better corresponds with the cycle of your incoming bills. The same rules apply to the monthly budget: Don't overspend, don't rob your savings account, and fatten that account by any means possible.

From our own experience, here's one caveat about monthly budgets: Because a month creates the feeling that there's more time to play with, it's easier to rationalize expenditures that aren't earmarked in the budget. You say to yourself, "Money will come from somewhere over the course of the month to cover that expense." Maybe it did once. Maybe you got lucky. So you'll get lucky again, won't you? Next thing you know, you're over budget and sliding down that slippery slope.

Use Budgets for Family Money Lessons

A final word about budgets: They're one of the best tools you have for educating your kids about money. Having the entire family participate in a "budget summit" once a week or month helps children understand the importance of making prudent financial decisions. In the most concrete way possible, budget meetings teach kids that the family money supply is finite and invests them in a we're-all-in-this-together spirit of decision making. Once a budget is agreed upon, don't bury it! Post it in a place where all family members can see it during the period when it's in effect.

How democratic should these budget meetings be? That answer will vary from family to family and according to the age and maturity of the children. But the bottom-line point is that there's no better way to teach kids about financial management and the central role of money in democratic government.

Take Back the "F" Word

It's okay—it really is. The ostentatious eighties are ancient history, and conspicuous consumption—Thorstein Veblen's famous phrase lambasting the in-your-face excesses of materialism—just ain't as cool as it used to be. It's okay to be frugal.

Being frugal is not to be confused with being cheap—with being ungenerous, miserly, Scrooge-like. The word *frugal*—which derives from a Latin root meaning "fit for food," thus worthy—evokes an honorable heritage, a centuries-old tradition of thriftiness, of bearing good fruit. In fact, the word *fruit* derives from a related root. To be frugal means to be a thoughtful—not a wasteful—consumer, to be smart about your purchases, and to get good value not only for yourself and your family but for the health of our planet. Frugality, as it did for my parents, can increase your ability to be generous to others, both with your time and your money.

Nick Bragg, our friend from Winston-Salem, North Carolina, enjoys ribbing me about being—in his words—"tight." Though it's all in good fun, I don't see it quite that way. To me, being thoughtful, being resourceful, with your money—no matter how large or small your bank account—just makes good common sense.

Over a decade ago in Maine, a feisty former graphic designer named Amy Dacyczyn launched a newsletter called *The Tightwad Gazette* and wrote a book of the same name. Billing herself as "the Frugal Zealot," Dacyczyn offered a grab bag of ideas on how to practice frugality, arguing that Americans had lost touch with their parents' and grandparents' practical financial wisdom.

Long before the book's publication, while still working outside the home, Dacyczyn had dreamed of having a big family, being a stay-at-home mom, and living in a large, old New England farmhouse. Conventional wisdom had it that she and her husband would have to continue in their professions to realize her dream, and that she could never be a full-time homemaker and mother.

That wisdom rankled Dacyczyn. Ultimately, she set about proving it wrong based on the principle of increasing savings, rather than increasing earnings. Her strategy was for her family—which included six children at the time her book was published—to live on her husband's income while spending as little as possible in every category of expenses. Dacyczyn recycled aluminum foil, dispensed with convenience foods, and discovered thousands of ways to cut expenses.

Ultimately, in less than seven years, living on an annual income averaging under thirty thousand dollars, the Dacyczyns bought and furnished their dream pre-1900 farmhouse (complete with attached barn), saved forty-nine thousand dollars, and were completely debt-free. Starting from zero at the time of their wedding, they realized their goals with a frugality few could—or would choose to—match.

Dacyczyn's story is instructive. Clearly, you don't have to be a zealot to grasp her basic notion that saving more—rather than earning more—can be a successful route to your goals.

It was for Wanda and me. Learning the value of frugality when we moved from Los Angeles to my family's debt-ridden Blue Ridge fruit orchard, we saved money for the first time as a couple, renovated an aging farmhouse, and paid off all debts. Motivated—like Dacyczyn—by the dream of a simpler life, we discovered the challenge—and fun—of living better on less.

Frugality, it's been suggested, is unpatriotic. What's patriotic, folks of this persuasion argue, is to shop and shop and shop, since roughly two-thirds of the American economy is driven by consumer spending. Without that spending, what would happen to our economy? these folks ask. What would happen to businesses and workers that rely on consumer spending for survival?

The answers are, of course, complex. Even economists disagree about the merits of spending versus saving. However, some have argued that a higher savings rate and less consumer debt—which frugal practices promote—would likely be beneficial to the economy. Juliet Schor notes in her book *The Overspent American* that our economy soared during the 1990s despite the "downshifting" of roughly one-fifth of the population. In fact, 30 percent of those "downshifters" cut their spending by half or more.

Schor agrees with conventional economic theory suggesting that when people consume less—and, as a corollary, usually work less—economic growth slows down. But she argues that this isn't necessarily a bad thing. She points to countries like the Netherlands and Denmark, which boast a large number of what she calls "postmaterialists." "In these countries, the slow growth rate merely means that people are not so intent on making a high income or consuming a lot," Schor observes. "As long as unemployment does not become a problem, slow (or no) growth is a perfectly acceptable reflection of people's choices and priorities. They prefer more time off from work. Or more environmental protection. They opt for more financial security. There is no economic commandment that says we must maximize the growth rate."

Europe, Schor suggests, is asking the right questions about consumption and economics. "Throughout Europe," she writes, "people are wondering whether the globalization of consumer markets isn't proceeding too rapidly, with too little thought. They are worried that they will not be able to maintain their quality of life in a world where making as much money as possible has become the reigning religion. And they are trying to find another way, a model of a decently functioning economy coexisting with a decent cultural and daily life experience. Isn't it time Americans started asking some of these same questions?"

As a business owner who's been a three-time president of our Carroll County (Virginia) Chamber of Commerce and has long served on the county's planning commission, the last thing I would advocate is that everyone take a vow of poverty and stop spending altogether. What I do champion—both as businessman and as consumer—is a self-disciplined approach to thoughtful purchasing based not on *wants* but on *needs*. The Madison Avenue mythology machine that tells you what you have is never good enough, the culture of credit cards, and the keeping-up-with-the-Joneses mind-set have conspired to make us feel inadequate if we don't spend money like the proverbial drunken sailor on shore leave. "Live for today!" is our financial rallying cry.

But it need not be that way.

Frugal Frank's Top Dozen Tips

Some of the things I've learned about frugality were passed on to me by my parents, Sam and Miriam Levering, Quaker orchardists and internationally known peace activists who raised five children and lived frugally for fifty-seven years of married life—and shared a lot of fun and laughter doing it.

From them, I also learned the importance of knowing *why* you're being frugal. Sam and Miriam had two major reasons. First, they wanted to trade income for time—primarily for their unpaid peace activism—so frugality was essential. Second, my mother in particular wanted to spend less on herself so that she'd have more money to help others. As the daughter of a Methodist minister, Mom had a heartfelt, Christian-based altruism that was a strong motivating force for her frugality.

That said, here are Frugal Frank's Top Dozen Tips, which have served us well in our efforts to *save* more money in order to *spend* more time leading richer lives. Remember, there are times when you'll want—and need—to modify some of these ideas. The point is not to achieve 100 percent consistency but to establish an overall pattern of frugality. And remember, too, that being frugal is not about self-aggrandizement. It's about priorities, generosity, and valuing our world as much as we value ourselves.

1. Buy used

Cars, clothes, appliances, computers, etc.—whenever possible, take advantage of the rapid decline in price once an item is no longer new. (A new car can depreciate more than 20 percent as soon as you leave the lot.) When buying used, make sure that a mechanic checks out your car before purchase, and be sure to road-test it. Check out all used appliances before purchase. Buy clothes at thrift shops, but be careful to check for rips, holes, and stains—and always try the clothes on. I recently found a pair of jeans I wanted at a thrift store and discovered that, once I had them on, the zipper wouldn't stay in place!

2. Eat lower on the food chain

Whatever you may think about meat, much of it is relatively expensive. Eating less or even no meat can reduce your food costs by at least 20 to 30 percent. The world of meatless meals is one of infinite variety, with flavors that meat-centric folks will never experience. And learning to cook without meat is one of the most fun things you'll ever do.

3. Grow you own food

Sure, it's time consuming, but so is anything that's really worth doing. Urban and suburban gardening is on the rise. And if you live in the country, why would you do anything else? Planting and tending a backyard orchard is very rewarding and relatively simple. Okay, you probably won't grow *all* your food, but why not experience the joy—and reap the savings—of growing some of it?

4. Take good care and make repairs

Maintaining what you have and repairing things instead of merely replacing them will usually save you money. In applying this wisdom of your grandparents to your vehicle, you can save thousands of dollars in gas consumption by getting regular tune-ups, maintaining proper tire pressure, etc. And once your vehicle is paid off, you won't constantly have to make payments, usually fattened by interest.

5. Buy a product for durability rather than novelty

When you do buy a new item—or even a used one—think about how long it will last. How well is it made? What are the materials used to make it? Will it age well as you yourself grow older? Will it stay in fashion?

6. Avoid status purchases

The power of advertising and of peer pressure can entice us to buy upscale products that project exclusivity—certain lines of clothing, cars, appliances, furniture, etc. Ask yourself why you are thinking of purchasing that BMW or Coach briefcase. Never buy anything—anything!—because you think it will make you feel more distinctive or more important. Make utility and value the primary motivations for your purchases.

7. Buy in bulk

With basic necessities like soap, toilet paper, canned foods, whole grains, etc., buying in bulk strikes a blow for frugality. Warehouse and discount stores and food co-ops are great places for bulk shopping. But don't forget the size of your storage spaces!

8. Bundle your errands

People living out in the country who come into town on shopping and other errands have been doing this forever. The rest of us can, too.

Hattie's Car-Buying Wisdom

Hattie Brintle, a dear friend of Wanda's and a certified public accountant, sees many of her clients—as well as her own two young-adult daughters—blow wads of money on cars and car payments. Often, Hattie comments wryly, people go car shopping and behave like kids in the proverbial candy store, overreaching and buying more expensive cars than they can afford. Hattie suggests to anyone who will listen a plan that will ensure financial manageability:

1. Pick out your dream car at a car lot

2. With the help of the car salesman, figure out what your payment would be

3. Go home and make this payment to yourself—into your savings account—every month for six months

This way, you'll see if you can afford the car payment. If you can't, you haven't lost a thing, and you'll understand that you need to find a less expensive vehicle. If you can, you'll have saved a hefty down payment.

"I also tell my daughters that once they find their car and pay it off, keep that car and make the 'car payments' to their savings accounts. This," she says, "is a sound strategy for saving for your retirement."

What does Hattie drive? "I'm still in my 1988 Acura Legend. My daughters tease me mercilessly, but I've got money in the bank."

With careful planning, it's amazing how much gas and time you can save by errand-bundling.

9. Examine your heating and cooling needs

Whenever you're warming or cooling your living space, you're spending plenty of money. What can you do to spend less? Is more heat escaping than necessary? Can you get by with less air conditioning—by using ceiling fans, for example? Air conditioning in a car decreases gas mileage by 15 percent. How often do you really, really need that colder air?

10. Trade services

Long an informal tradition in rural areas like ours—I regularly trade services with neighbors—bartering has become institutionalized in some American cities. What skills do you have that might be exchanged for someone else's?

11. Take adventurous—not expensive—vacations

My parents were the masters of this art, taking the family on vivid camping trips all over the United States and keeping our bellies happy on peanut-butter-and-jelly sandwiches! If you can't abide the thought of a sleeping bag or a national park, try clean, low-priced motels and all the free (or relatively inexpensive) pleasures many cities have to offer: museums, public parks, beaches, etc.

12. Create your own entertainment

We've probably taken this idea to an extreme—by starting our outdoor Cherry Orchard Theatre!—but you get the idea. Why not do fun, entertaining stuff that's free or inexpensive—touch football, anyone? a storytelling contest with friends or family?—instead of relying exclusively on commercial entertainment that's often not all it's cracked up to be? "Entertainment," in a sense, also applies to eating at restaurants. It's not only the food but the atmosphere that we pay for when we dine out. Here's a simple rule of thumb: As much as possible, dine out only when you're celebrating something. Make dining out a special occasion. Call me a Grinch if you like, but eating home-cooked meals saves a lot of money—and if you're a good cook, they're tastier and healthier, too.

Live in Less Space

Whatever happened to the idea of living spaces designed on a human scale? Why do we need the humongous houses many of us live in already or that are under construction, houses with thousands of square feet and with rooms that dwarf their human inhabitants? "Americans," as Millard Fuller, founder with his wife, Linda, of Habitat for Humanity, once told Wanda and me at his modest house in Americus, Georgia, "are seriously overhoused."

Here's a big money-saving suggestion: If you are overhoused, consider downsizing to a smaller home. Pocket the money you'll save—big money, very likely—and put it to personally meaningful use. If you're living in a modest space but are feeling tempted to "upscale" to larger quarters, carefully weigh the financial—and psychic—costs.

Be a "Free" Thinker

It would be unfrugal (not to mention unfruitful) of me not to reserve a special section for the whole idea of free activities in a simpler life. Given the mainstream belief that money stands in direct proportion to value, the very idea of things that are both free and valuable seems almost counterintuitive, if not radical.

A sunset, of course. Wind in a willow tree. Those intangible free things we all experience.

But here are some other ideas. All the books, magazines, and videos available for free at your library. Riding on a bike path. Playing basketball on a public court. Jogging in a park.

This list could go on forever. The fact that something is free says nothing negative about its quality. All that's required is a little imagination—and an open mind.

Escape Credit-Card Hell

They arrive in the mailbox almost daily: credit-card offers that conjure up romantic fantasies of a life without limits. Who's sending these valentines from La-La Land? Check the return address carefully. I do believe it's that curious chap sporting the pitchfork and horns.

If there's a single financial problem that's public enemy number one, it's the temptation to live on credit. Credit cards make that trap all too easy to fall into. According to the 2004 *State of the World* report from Worldwatch Institute,

61 percent of American credit-card holders have an outstanding balance each month, and the average credit-card debt exceeds twelve thousand dollars. I know, I know, you can't escape the damned things—not if you want to rent a car, for example. But you can do what tens of millions of Americans are failing to do: you can "drink" in moderation. Easier said than done? Certainly, but here are three tips for making credit cards work for you instead of vice versa:

1. Limit yourself to one

Contrary to what you'll read in every new offer, life gets simpler with only one credit card. You've got it when you need it, but you don't have to deal with all the devilish temptations—and subsequent bill paying—of multiple cards.

2. Don't take it with you

No kidding. If impulse or binge credit-card use is a problem, leave the card at home except when you know you'll need it. Put it in a drawer. Bury it under old photographs of ex-boyfriends or something! Or as Janet Luhrs suggests, freeze your card in water so it will take time to thaw!

3. Pay off your debt

Sell your firstborn—do whatever it takes to get out from under those usurious interest payments. Go without food three days a week and apply those savings—anything! Credit-card companies speak with honeyed tongues when they're romancing you, but, man, do they stick that knife in when you're in the hole. Enjoy playing poker with the devil and his deck of cards? Get in credit-card debt and that's pretty much the story.

Lower the "Pulse" Rate of Impulse Buys

Daniel Gilbert, the lively Harvard psychology professor who studies happiness, made an off-the-cuff, yet fundamental, remark in our conversation with him. The subject wasn't happiness. It was shopping.

"Remember," he said with a grin, "the retailer's problem is that you have money that they haven't gotten from you yet. The way they are going to design a store is a way designed to maximize the transfer of wealth from your pocketbook to theirs."

Of course, Gilbert was right, as we all know. But we're seduced anyway, adroitly lured into impulse buys by savvy retailers. You can't blame them, just as you can't blame the spider for trapping the fly in her web. Everyone has to eat. But you can play the seduction game and win.

Delay Purchases

Wanda has more interest in clothes than I do, so she's developed some sound strategies for keeping her buying under control.

Let's say, like Wanda, you fall in love with a pair of shoes. You didn't walk into the store thinking you were going to buy shoes, but there they are, and it's love at first sight. Your pulse rate is going bonkers!

Don't buy now. Buy only what's on your list. Go home, find your calendar, and write the word *shoes* on the date a week from now.

A lot can happen in a week. In this case, it's all good. In all likelihood, by delaying your purchase, you slowed your pulse rate. Good. It's even possible that you've completely forgotten about those magic shoes you thought you couldn't live without. That's good, too. Or you go to the store and the shoes are gone, in which case you've saved the money. Good. Or if you can't get those shoes off your mind, and, more importantly, you really could use them in your wardrobe, *and* you can afford them, then buy them with a clear conscience. You've made a thoughtful purchase, not an impulse buy you may later regret.

To Borrow or Not to Borrow? That Is the Question

Ralph Levering, my bearded Quaker grandfather, who, along with my grandmother Clara, founded our orchard in 1908, was a real prohibitionist when it came to borrowing money. "Pay as you go" was his strict financial credo. He was a reluctant lender as well. Any tools borrowed by neighbors from his toolshed had to be returned to their exact places by nightfall the same day.

In the 1930s, FDR's Works Progress Administration commenced construction of the Blue Ridge Parkway, which now runs just two miles above our orchard. Ralph Levering opposed the project, linking it to the overarching horror (as he saw it) of Roosevelt's federal deficit spending.

As it turned out, the Blue Ridge Parkway is arguably the best thing that ever happened to our Orchard Gap neighborhood. But my grandfather's pay-as-you-go philosophy has a great deal to be said for it. My father, who borrowed money liberally for the orchard for thirty-five years, jeopardized its future by incurring more debt load than the business could carry. This is, perhaps, the twenty-twenty wisdom of hindsight. But it created family stress for many years and was a thorn in the side of our large family's honest experiment in simple living.

Given this sort of background, it's small wonder that I feel inclined to paraphrase Hamlet on the subject of money borrowing. Can borrowing money simplify your life? Ah, that is the question! Of course it can, any bank will tell you. Or does it—as Thoreau or my grandfather would tell you—undermine the very foundation of a simpler life?

The answer is that there's no simple answer! And it's also true that these questions have somewhat different applications in business, government, and education, in which borrowing undeniably can help pave the way for success. But I do think the slippery-slope principle rears its head again.

Borrowing money is a bit like crossing the crevasses as you climb Mount Rainier in Washington State, as I did in my twenties. Here's my own, modified Ralph Levering rule on the subject: Exercise *extreme* caution. If you need to borrow—as most of us do, from time to time—do it only as a last resort. And once you do it, borrow the lowest amount you can, and pay it back as quickly as you can. When I enrolled at Harvard Divinity School two years out of college, it's true that I took out a student loan. But I also had savings I could apply to tuition, and I worked two jobs while enrolled in school.

So there it is—borrowing's a situational thing. It's also full of risk. The risk is that, for one reason or another, you'll keep borrowing until the cows come home—and when exactly will those recalcitrant cows be coming on home? For a variety of reasons—as the millions who've declared personal bankruptcy the past few years can attest—seemingly manageable debt can snowball. And even if it doesn't, the relentless stress of debt can send Hamlet's "slings and arrows" straight into the heart of the simple life. Whenever you possibly—*possibly*—can, pay as you go. I think the bearded Quaker had an enduring point.

Invest Your Values

This one, I'll keep short. Getting debt off your back sure lightens the load! Once that load is off, the mind takes wing and begins a serious look at what financial oracles love to call "investment opportunities." Though Wanda and I have made stock-market investments (which are by no means incompatible with a simpler life), we do favor relatively cautious choices. Unless you can afford to lose big bucks, this approach may help you, like us, to sleep well at night. Your returns may well be modest, but meanwhile, life is good in direct proportion to the number of things you have to worry about.

The larger issue, for us, is value based. Investments, we think, should reflect core values. Here's a simple, tried-and-true "pass-along": Invest in enterprises or stocks that you really do believe in, not for their get-rich potential but for their ultimate worth to your community or country. Simplicity and conscience are two peas in a pod. Take time to do the research. Is there a gap between words and actions? Then, if the investment checks out, put your money to work! And diversify, diversify, diversify!

Money, You, and a Simpler Life

Let's return, full circle, to the question with which we started: What is your relationship with money?

I want to be perfectly blunt here. Money—at least as we deal with it as individuals—is not brain surgery. True, the issues get more complicated if you want to make more and more and more money—clearly not a great idea if you're really trying to simplify your life. And for making more and more money, the woods are full of experts fairly roaring with advice! They sell zillions of books. In lectures, advice columns, magazine articles, and television sound bites, they tell us how to be "secure" by being wealthier. They pursue—by methods that are often more complicated than they are telling us—an illusory, money-based happiness that both recent scientific research and many centuries of common experience reveal has no basis in reality.

But with personal finances, let there be no mistake: The basics really are the basics. An older generation that lived through the Depression learned those basics: Know what your resources are; stick to your budget; be frugal; always look for bargains; save as much money as you can; borrow as little as you can; get out of debt as fast as you can.

It's hardly rocket science. Yet somehow, something happened on the way to the American dream. What was it? Somehow, we lost sight of elementary truths that have always made good financial sense, becoming a nation in serious hock, from the individual to the government level. Somehow, we lost our perspective on how much is enough.

Self-discipline is everything. When it comes to money, I can't overemphasize the importance of knowing yourself and keeping on the financial straight and narrow. It's what we teach our children—or should teach them—so why can't we practice self-discipline ourselves?

To do that, we may sometimes have to resort to extreme measures. Can't resist impulse buys at the mall or upscale shops? Then by all means avoid malls and upscale shops! Have a hard time not ordering a pricey item from a catalog? Then toss that catalog straight from the mailbox into your recycling bin! Go into a buying frenzy when in the company of big-spending friends? Then socialize with them less, or don't go shopping with them! Can't resist the lure of slick television advertising? Then turn off the TV set or mute the commercials! Tend to go shopping when you're feeling depressed? Then monitor your state of mind, recognize the warning signals, and find alternatives to addictive shopping habits!

Don't stand on your pride. Whatever it takes to practice financial self-discipline, do it. As Alex Gibbs, my old Mount Airy High School football coach, used to say, "No excuses. Just get it done."

The difficult challenge, then, is that of will power. It's a bit like losing weight. Despite all the ballyhoo about the "right" diets, there's really no great mystery to losing weight: Eat the right foods in the right proportion and get plenty of exercise. Just basic stuff. Summon your will power, and the rest will take care of itself.

It's the same with money. By sticking with the basics, your relationship with money can be a healthy one. The biggest challenge with money and simplicity is not brain power, but rather the will to do what you need to do. It's having the heart.

CHAPTER 3

Love Your Work, Love Your Life

*"What seems important to me is not what a person does,
but how they do it."*

—George Peck

"Work," the irrepressible English playwright Oscar Wilde once remarked, "is more fun than fun."

Well, maybe it was for Oscar Wilde. And, I have to admit, it is sometimes fun for Wanda and me, particularly when our work as writers and fruit orchardists leads us to stimulating people and interesting new challenges.

For most of us these days, though, work is still work and fun—if we can find time for it—is still fun, and never the twain shall meet. According to a recent poll conducted by the National Opinion Research Center at the University of Chicago, less than half of American workers are even "moderately satisfied" with their jobs. A survey by Princeton Research Associates reports that three-fourths of American employees believe that workers experience more on-the-job stress than a generation ago. Are we having fun yet?

If you're lucky enough to have a job—and many of us aren't so lucky—chances are that not only is work not fun, but there's also too much of it. Americans work more hours than do citizens of any other industrialized country. On average, we work 1,878 hours annually. Sound like a lot? Well, to put it in perspective, that's about nine full weeks more than workers in Western Europe. According to Boston College professor Juliet Schor, author of *The Overworked American*, "the amount of time Americans have spent at their jobs has risen steadily" since the late 1960s, and continues to rise. For many of us, fifty-plus-hour work weeks are the norm, a

Sisyphean load exacerbated by unpaid work at home. With women now comprising nearly half the American work force—while still doing the lion's share of work at home—you have to wonder just when body and soul will be forced to shout, "Enough already!" "Women, especially," Schor observes ruefully, "have lost time for self."

"Self time"—that is, time for leisure, for new learning opportunities and spiritual growth—is not the only casualty of too many work hours. The epidemic of overwork attacks our health, our families, our community life.

Stress and obesity. Absentee-parent families. Uninformed citizens who may or may not vote and in other ways fortify democracy. All these ills and more can be linked in large measure to overwork in a society that's simply run out of time. Time to exercise. Time to do your own thinking. Even the devastating erosion of environmental quality is tied to overwork; studies show that time-stressed Americans are more likely to use throwaway products and less likely to find time to recycle.

Whatever happened on the way to the good life? Back in the 1950s, as Boomers were merrily emerging from their diapers, many Americans believed we were on the verge of a golden era of leisure and short work weeks. Indeed, we *were* working fewer hours in the fifties. And with all those beguiling new gadgets—those "labor-saving" devices—at our disposal, many of us looked forward to a new age in which work would not occupy the bulk of our time. Sure, there was the Bomb to worry about. But work? What, me worry?

And so we didn't. But what happened was that worker productivity rose dramatically on a per-hour basis, particularly in the period after 1973, when it nearly doubled. "In effect," writes John de Graaf, co-author of *Affluenza*, in the *New York Times*, "the United States as a society took all of its increases in labor productivity in the form of money and stuff instead of time." In other words, we traded our nonwork time—our priceless selves outside the workplace—for the devil's own reward in the form of greater and greater material prosperity.

Schor calls this bargain with ol' Lucifer "the work-and-spend cycle." Along with the overload in work hours demanded by many employers, "what's happened is that people's material needs or expectations, the lifestyles that they want to attain, have moved along with those hours. So that it's a combination—I call it 'the work-and-spend cycle'—of, 'You gotta work the long hours to keep the job, you need the job to maintain the lifestyle.' And it becomes a kind of self-reinforcing cycle."

Schor herself fell prey to the cycle she describes. "There was a time," she told Wanda in her Boston home, "when I worked very long hours. But that was before I had children." Like many middle-aged moms at once in the workplace and raising children, Schor faced the challenge of how simultaneously to keep her job *and* create more family time.

Her solution? Downshifting. "Since I've changed my life, sort of downshifted to a less consumerist lifestyle," she said, "I have put much more thought into the things that I buy." At the same time, she reduced her work hours by focusing on greater efficiency. "Now," she said, "I'm more productive and intense when I'm at the office because I spend a lot less time there."

Workplace Yearnings

Just imagine, a life like Juliet Schor's with shorter work hours and time for the (real) good life, for life beyond the rat race—perhaps a more evocative description of Schor's work-and-spend cycle. Dream for a moment. Climb out of that rat costume—it doesn't flatter you. Ask yourself a simple question: "What do I *really* want from work?" Then sit down and make a list.

Here's my "want" list from the work I do as orchardist, writer, and producer. See if this strikes a chord.

1. Financial stability

I don't want to have to worry all the time about where the money is going to come from next week or next year. My work doesn't need to make me rich, but it does need to help create a steady-as-she-goes feeling aboard my financial ship.

2. Satisfying, meaningful work in line with my values and sense of purpose

I want my work to be challenging—to keep me learning and stretching—and at the same time to be beneficial to others and to the environment.

3. The right balance

I want neither too much work nor too little, with ample time for other things that are important.

Is that too much to ask? Why should it be? Imagine, if you will, a life in which there's *real* time for family—not stolen, guilt-ridden "quality time," one of the hollowest phrases of our era. Imagine a life with your finances in order. A life that has time to breathe—time for working on your soul, for giving back to your community and country. Imagine, therefore, a life in which you don't need as much money, because what spending *less* does is give you *more* room to maneuver in the workplace.

It's a daydream many share. According to a national survey conducted by the

Radcliffe Public Policy Center, 61 percent of Americans say they would be willing to give up some of their salary for more time with the kids or other family members. The same survey reports that a whopping 82 percent of men ages twenty-one through thirty-nine "rated family time as their top priority, breaking ranks with their fathers and grandfathers on work-family issues." Of those younger men, 71 percent said they would trade income for family time, a figure 10 percent higher than the general population.

"Young men," observes Paula Reymen, the center's director, "are beginning to replicate women's sensibilities—instead of women in the workplace trying to be more like men."

Such findings offer hope for a new, less work-centric era, an era not unlike the one envisioned in the 1950s. But how do we get there? What can one person in a work-driven culture do?

You Are Not Your Work

It seems self-evident. Who among us truly believes that what we "do"—our work—is who we are?

Yet go to any party and what's the first question a stranger asks? "So, what do you do?"

Try answering, "What do I *do*? I live."

Live?

But it's true. Your identity and your self-esteem cannot be measured by the work you do, can they?

If your answer is a truthful "Yes, they can," there's work to do. No, not at work. There's work to be done with the voice inside you that, if you are listening, will steer

---

Balancing Acts: Frank and Suzanne Spence

The Frank Spence I know has always had an artistic streak. For thirteen years, I taught an adult writing class at Surry Community College in Dobson, North Carolina. "Dr. Frank," as I sometimes called him, graced a number of those classes with his ingenious stories, philosophical essays, and flashing wit. Seeing Frank arrive in class—with or without his physician's pager—always gave me a lift. I knew that a friend and a contemporary was going to spend the next three hours with me, someone who'd laugh at my preening puns and nod his handsome head in solidarity when I groped my way through a maze of particularly tortuous prose.

What I didn't know about Frank was the artistry he would apply to his own life. Nearly a decade ago, Frank and his wife, Suzanne, the parents of two youngish children, jointly fired Frank's work life and redesigned the family configuration. From now on, the family practitioner with the sixty- to seventy-hour work weeks would have time with his wife and kids, take long meditative walks, learn to play the guitar, study Spanish, and hunker down with Suzanne in the kitchen preparing exotic vegan dishes the likes of which you've never tasted.

I make that last statement from table-level experience. On a crisp November day, I drove from nearby Mount Airy to Frank and Suzanne's modest home in Elkin, North Carolina. I came, I saw, and I dined. And when that spicy vegetable-and-tofu stir-fry settled peaceably in my belly, I listened as Frank and Suzanne wrote the book—out loud—on how to balance work with the other things that matter.

Something, it seems clear to them now, had to give. Frank's grueling work hours coupled with the demands of raising a son and daughter laid down the fault lines for a potential earthquake in the Spence house. "I dreaded going to work," Frank remembered. "It was too much, too intense. I could never relax. And there was never enough time to recover from it."

The burden of parenting James and Caitlyn was falling primarily on Suzanne, an interior designer who'd called a time-out on her career in order to have more time with her kids. "Frank's patience," she remembered of that period, "was very thin with the children. He'd come home exhausted and essentially just want me to deal with them. I'd been with the kids all day, and, well, I'd had enough of them."

Somehow—the time and place are lost to memory now—a series of urgent conversations commenced between Frank and Suzanne. "Everybody," Suzanne remarked tersely, "has to decide what they can take. And that's where we started."

"I had to do something," Frank said. "The situation was physically painful for me. I was gonna go nuts. I had a good job, I was making good money, but that's not all there is to it. My life meant more to me than the extra money."

With full support from Suzanne, as well as from his physician partner, who likewise yearned for a simpler life, Frank withdrew from his family practice and steered toward his goal: a twenty- to thirty-hour work week. Over time, the composition of that work week emerged: part-time work in urgent care in nearby Statesville and a one-day-a-week job at the Surry County Health Department in Dobson.

Frank's reviews of both jobs are raves. He loves the camaraderie of the group with whom he works in urgent care, and the job at the health department has immersed him in the culturally rich waters of the Latino community, whose numbers have increased exponentially in Surry County in the past decade. And with a gentler work load, Frank's passion for the "bliss" of medicine has returned.

"I like medicine a lot more than I did," he told me flatly. "I'm reading about it every day. I *want* to spend time learning about things I'm seeing. Overall, I'm just much happier now. I really do enjoy medicine."

Reducing his work hours gave Frank the time for another pleasure-giver—learning Spanish. He taught himself using Berlitz tapes as well as real-life encounters with Spanish-language speakers. At the health department, he recalled, his Latino patients were "very forgiving" as he learned their language. "Every effort I made was welcomed and encouraged." As Frank gained proficiency, "people would ask, 'Where did you live in Mexico?' I took that as a compliment!" Nowadays, he carries on full-scale conversations with his patients, the days long gone when Latino children acted as interpreters for their parents in Frank's office.

His balanced new life bore fruit on the home front as well. Frank's time and energy for parenting were, he and Suzanne agree, among the most gratifying developments in their marriage. Having time for James and Caitlyn was highly satisfying. Frank also tackled his long-term dream of learning to play the guitar, and he found more time for his old passion of reading and writing on philosophical topics. There was time as well for serious daily walking, an activity Frank shares with Suzanne and which both say brings physical and mental-health benefits. Their hour-long walks together, Frank said, are great marriage-bonders.

But what about income? Having known the Spences a long time, I understood they weren't lavish spenders, never driving expensive cars and choosing to live for many years in an old house on Main Street they'd renovated when they moved to Elkin from Florida. Still, James and Caitlyn are in college now. Hadn't the reduced work hours created a degree of financial stress?

As a matter of fact, *no*. Frank's income, it turns out, is comparable to what it was during his sixty-hours-a-week period, though he told me that if he'd stayed in his family practice over the past ten years, his income would have risen sharply. So, in essence, what Frank gave up was that even-greater affluence that comes with trading your life for money.

Was his trade worth it? "Well," he said, "we don't feel materially deprived at all. We don't need all the fancy stuff that's available to you when you're making a huge amount of money. I mean, when you think about it, Americans like us are at the top of the heap, when you think about the world."

Frank and Suzanne are anything but smug about the choices they've made. They understand that not everyone earns a doctor's salary, that the comfortable middle-class lifestyle they maintain is not so readily achieved by cutting your work hours when your earning power is not that of a physician.

Still, Frank remains convinced that a healthy balance between work and life is more achievable than many folks can see from a vantage point inside Juliet Schor's "work-and-spend cycle." "I think if you have a strong enough desire to make changes, you need to look and find opportunities to make those changes," Frank said. "And often, the opportunities are there."

Frank found his, and he has no regrets. "I think cutting back on my work hours was one of the most important things I've done in my life," he said. "It was a big change for me and my family—and I wouldn't change it for anything."

you to a larger sense of who you are. As Marie Sherlock asks rhetorically, "Are we human beings or human doings?" The first step in finding a balance between work and the rest of your life is to shed the idea that you and your work are synonymous.

That's easier said than done, but not impossible by any means. Here are three things you can do to get started:

1. Keep a journal

Buy a notebook and get in the habit of recording regular, written reflections on what you find meaningful in your life outside of work. Begin to assess in written form the value of a spouse, a child, a book in your life. By writing these assessments down, you invest in their value and etch that value into your mind.

2. Look for one or more things to do outside of work that you suspect would interest you

Particularly if you're a classic workaholic—i.e., there is no meaning outside of work—take up a hobby, volunteer in your community, set aside regular time to read fiction. Whatever it is you think might be of interest, do it and do it now!

3. Surprise yourself and others by vocalizing your values

The next time someone asks, "So, what do you do?" reply with something like this: "Well, I do a lot of things. I read good books like _____. I spend some amazing evenings with my _____. I mentor a twelve-year-old student down at _____." Somewhere in this spiel, you can also mention the work you do. Get the idea? Sure, it's semi-obnoxious, but only because the person who asked the question may take it as a wise-guy answer—initially, at any rate. What it will do, though, is affirm your new way of seeing yourself. To say it out loud is to begin to believe it! And it will cause that person—who is probably work driven, too, and is probably trying to figure out if he or she is more "successful" than you—to stop for a moment and consider the merits of the point you are making. With luck, it will even lead to a truly meaningful conversation, instead of just another my-job's-more-significant-than-yours exchange, often the subtext of work-oriented conversations.

These three ideas have worked for me at one time or another. You may have another approach. Whatever it takes, the point is to learn to see yourself as having a multidimensional identity. Put your work self in perspective. It is only one piece of your total identity.

Leaving Debt, USA

So you're on the edge of town, driving down the highway, and a sign looms ahead:

LEAVING DEBT, USA
POPULATION: ZILLIONS
DON"T HURRY BACK!

How would you respond? Would you turn around and—out of sheer perversity—hurry right back into town? Or would you keep on rolling, happy to get that madhouse metropolis behind you?

Seems like a no-brainer, doesn't it? But sometimes the most important choices we *don't* make are the ones right in front of our noses. That's the way it is with debt. To be in debt, many of us assume, is as American as apple pie. The average American household, after all, is in hock twelve thousand dollars or so in credit-card debt alone. Debt? In our buy-now, pay-later consumer culture, what's the big deal about debt?

In chapter 2, in discussing borrowing, my bottom-line advice was to proceed with extreme caution. And if you must borrow, pay off your debt as quickly as possible. This is particularly true when you consider debt's impact on workplace options. Arguably, the steepest price of debt comes on the job. Carrying a heavy debt load limits your work options, robs you of freedom and flexibility. Surveys show that debt is the number-one reason most of us are afraid to reduce our work hours. "I owe, I owe, it's off to work I go," says that bumper sticker on the car ahead of you in the beautiful downtown morning gridlock. So much for freedom of choice.

And that's exactly the point: It may be right in front of our noses, but debt is something we *choose.* Once chosen, it's a slippery slope into deeper and deeper debt, as over a million personal bankruptcies a year attest in our Promised Land of milk, honey, and credit. But if we choose debt, we can also choose to get out of it, or not to get into it in the first place.

Getting out of debt can certainly be a steep climb. When Wanda and I moved to Levering Orchard in 1986 from Los Angeles, it took us six years to retire the debt on the farm, which had essentially become our personal debt. We worked long hours, particularly during the harvest months. We made it our goal to get out of debt as quickly as possible so that, once debt-free, we could downsize the orchard operation and work fewer hours. Looking back, we believe we made the right long-term decision, but we paid the short-term price of working more hours than we really desired. Life in the Blue Ridge Mountains remained sweet as a tree-ripe cherry, but it would have been sweeter still without that debt.

The bottom line: Want to downsize your work hours? The first thing to look at: The debt in your life. It's right in front of that big schnoz.

Pop the Big Question

If work is like the high-diving events at the Summer Olympics—demanding, scary, incredibly competitive—don't underestimate the degree of difficulty when you try to reduce your hours. "Work norms," Juliet Schor observes, "go along with jobs. So that it's very difficult for most people, in the job they have, to cut back their hours. That's not to say there's no ability to set limits."

Is your employer open to a reduction in your work hours? It's certainly worth finding out. While the reality is that many employers are not, it's also true that options like *job sharing*—in which you and other workers divide the hours of one job—are increasingly available at some companies.

Particularly if you're a highly skilled, highly desirable employee, you may have more power to negotiate than your employer will voluntarily divulge. According to Schor, "I think working less hours is a little bit easier for people with families, because there's more awareness among management that parents or others with family responsibilities somehow deserve more time."

Fire Your Job

Let's say the answer is no. *Nyet.* Sorry, Mary Sue, but the whole point of working for *our* company is to work yourself to death! *Karoshi*, it's called in Japan—literally, death from overwork. Often, relatively young Japanese workers simply keel over and die.

You have two options. Hang onto that job with blood, sweat, and bile, as millions of us do. Or fire it—use your noggin, your ingenuity, and refuse to take no for an answer when the subject is *your* happiness.

"Fire my job? That's easy for you to say!" you protest. And that's true, up to a point.

But consider what's at stake. And remember that perhaps you're more resourceful than you realize. Most of us are, when confronted with the imperative of change.

Clearly, before you fire your job, you'll need a game plan, a survival strategy for the next phase of your life. You'll need a budget—a financial road map for the transition from one job to another—as well as a firm grip on the financial resources available to you when you embark. Sure, it would be nice to know exactly where you're going to land before you make that leap. Maybe you have a new job lined up, or you're starting a small business. But if that sort of precision landing isn't in the cards—and, heaven knows, sometimes it's not—make that leap anyway if you have confidence in your abilities. Don't let your life pass you by!

Downshifting: Small Is Big

The decade of the 1990s witnessed a significant trend that continues unabated in the new millennium: *downshifting*. Millions of Americans have found ways to work less, simplifying their lives by choosing from a menu of options that often includes not only changing jobs but changing careers as well. In an era of home offices and telecommuting, *downshifters* have discovered the power of thinking small.

Often, of course, downshifters earn less than they did before the change. And in some cases, the change can limit career mobility. But the upside is compelling—not only a reduced work load, but greater flexibility for meeting family and personal needs.

Two strategies for downshifting merit serious consideration:

1. Self-employment

Today, some 15 million Americans—13 percent of the work force—are self-employed. When Wanda and I moved to the orchard from Los Angeles, we took the self-employment plunge sink-or-swim style, with no Plan B, and kept our heads well above water. Self-employment isn't for everyone. The buck stops with you, which for some folks piles on more stress than they can tolerate.

But—varying by degree according to the nature of the work—self-employment can offer more flexibility and more real independence than any other form of work. If you link it with reduced spending, as we did, self-employment more than pays the bills and creates a spaciousness in your life unlike anything you've ever experienced.

2. Part-time work

Again, this downshifting strategy works best with a full-court press to limit spending. But short of opting out of work entirely, for anyone getting serious about honoring nonwork priorities, part-time employment is the ultimate diet for work obesity.

Part-timers certainly face their share of challenges, ranging from (in some cases) less desirable jobs to lower hourly wages (and fewer or no benefits) than those of full-timers. In our national cult of work, we tend to stigmatize part-time labor as somehow a diminishment of our highest purpose in life. Certainly, if Prestige, Status, and Career Track are the three pillars of your philosophy, part-time work will never be the choice for you. But if you're serious about parenting, creativity, spirituality, and other forms of bona fide work, part-timing is the downshifter's gold standard.

Kings for Every Day

When neither self-employment nor part-time work is the solution to your workplace "winter of discontent," consider looking into an employee-owned company. Can 14 million workers be wrong? Roughly, that's the number of American employees who own a stake in their companies. What do Avis, United Parcel Service, Kroger, and United Airlines have in common? Many, though not all, of their employees are kings—or at least princes and princesses.

So what's the bottom line about co-owning your company? At their best, employee-owned companies offer some degree of democracy and equitable profit sharing. The folks actually doing the work play a key role in determining the company's mission, how the work is done, and where the profits go. At the same time, employees shoulder the responsibilities and risks of ownership—a double-edged sword that's not for everyone.

Whether or not working for an employee-owned company will simplify your life is debatable. What it may well do, however, is enhance your satisfaction at work. This is particularly true at companies where employees and managers work cooperatively from a joint vision of the company's mission, where there's a genuinely democratic management structure rather than the same old top-down flow of power.

Promotions, Promotions

Ladders are an integral part of my work. The ones I use are made out of wood and vary in length from fourteen to twenty-four feet. During our fruit harvests, you're likely to see me lugging these ladders around the orchard, climbing them, and setting them for customers in cherry, peach, and apple trees. But necessary as they are, they're also heavy and—by the end of the day—exhausting.

For me, then, climbing the corporate ladder has more than metaphorical resonance. Viscerally, when I hear the word *ladder*, I have mixed feelings. Yes, climbing a ladder is good, but there's also a steep price to be paid for doing it.

When you're promoted in a job (with apologies to Martha Stewart), that's a "good thing," isn't it? You're climbing that ladder. You'll likely earn more money, and you'll certainly be viewed by many with greater respect. But at what price glory (and money)? Particularly for managers and professionals, the price can be a fifty-plus-hour work week. The price is more stress, more travel, more daydreaming about "quality time" at home as you stare at your laptop at thirty thousand feet or wander off mentally in the boardroom.

"All junior executives should know," observes John Capozzi, "is that if they work hard ten hours a day, every day, they could be promoted to senior executives so that they can work hard for fourteen hours a day."

Think long and hard about that promotion. Don't jump on it before some heartfelt conversations with the home folks in your life. Are your children still young? Where will those kids be when the years you spend climbing the ladder are gone? Perhaps for you the price is worth it. But do yourself a favor by carefully considering it first.

Oil and Water

His patience wearing thin, our son, Henry, presses his head against a kitchen counter, waiting yet again for one of my patented science lessons. As a boy on a farm, why not start him now?

At the age of six, Henry does well to clear his eyes just over the top of the counter. I've placed a glass bowl there where my son can get a close look.

"Henry," I say, "check this out, kid!"

From one pitcher, I pour safflower oil. From another, I pour water on top of the unyielding oil. Henry's big brown eyes, peering over the countertop, grow bigger still as he watches the golden oil and the clear water do their I-am-what-I-am-and-you-are-not thing.

"Henry!" I proclaim. "Whaddaya know? Oil and water do not mix!"

Neither do work and life at home. Though it's difficult these days, particularly with children in your home, it's essential to set boundaries between the workplace and the home front.

Invading your home with work—whether bringing it home or letting it spill over from your home-based business—violates fundamental compacts between you and your significant other, you and your kids, and you and yourself. Work, the clear message is, is more important even than loved ones.

Check that work at your front door, or at the door of your home office. When it just isn't possible to do that, consider changing jobs.

Electronic (Un)Leashing

Isn't technology *mahvelous!* These days, unless you're a Luddite living off the grid, it's virtually impossible that you regard our glorious gizmos as anything less than indispensable. E-mail. Cell phones. Whiz-bang computers. Pagers. Whatever the latest technology is, it's touted to us by companies and colleagues alike as not only indispensable but time saving.

Did someone say *time saving?* Whose time? Yours? Mine? If all these devices save time, then why do we have *less* time, even within the workplace itself?

I don't mean to be a technology-basher here. But I do think it's "time" to get real.

Our devices giveth, and our devices taketh away. In the context of work, the bulk of the rhetoric is one sided: Technology (no, not love) is a many-splendored thing. Period. But more than that, technology—particularly in the form of the "electronic leash"—offers workers more ways to be model employees. These techno gadgets are nice status symbols for employees, too. Does the company benefit from hitching said employees to electronic leashes? Do bears like honey?

A word of warning: Being offered goodies like cell phones and pagers by your employer is a bit like those weirdly cheerful old ladies in *Arsenic and Old Lace* offering you tea. Maybe you won't perish, but now, more than ever, you'll belong to your employer. You're accessible anywhere, anytime. The boundary between your life and the life of the company has broken down, and you're plugged in "wirelessly" to your work.

The moral of this story? Beware of work-centric leashes. If you are unduly leashed already, unleash yourself without delay. The boundary you save just might be your own.

Getting There (and Back) Is Half the Fun

When Wanda and I lived in Los Angeles, our work—Wanda's as a newspaper reporter and editor, mine as a screenwriter and freelance journalist—swept us inexorably down miles and miles of car-choked asphalt, 'neath spacious, smog-draped skies. "Oh, what a beautiful morning!" we did not croon when we went off to work. "You know, honey, I feel fresh as a daisy!" we did not exclaim to each other at the end of another beautiful commute in paradise.

Sound familiar? The average American commute (there and back) is forty-five minutes. Millions of people commute literally hours a day. For Wanda, driving twenty miles to and from downtown L.A. (yes, Virginia, there *is* a downtown L.A.!) in rush-hour traffic, it was typically an hour and a half. My commute varied, depending on which of my many employers over a seven-year period required my illustrious services.

"I *drive*, therefore I am" is a primary credo of our cult of work, and not just in car-crazed L.A. Unless you think vitriolic talk-radio hosts and traffic updates are made in heaven, there has to be a better way to live. Here are five alternatives:

1. Telecommute

With the job you have, is it possible to let that computer do the commuting? (Yes, technology can be beautiful.) Maybe not every day, but some days? This is an alternative well worth looking into.

2. Change your work hours

This is not always easy, of course, but if you can find a way to avoid rush-hour traffic, the wear-and-tear factor should diminish considerably. This goes, too, for carpooling or using mass transit. These options are not always available, but when they are, go for it.

3. Find work closer to where you live

This is another option in the easier-said-than-done department, but then again, consider the impact on your heart of forty years of two-hour-a-day commutes. Remember *karoshi*, death from overwork?

4. Conversely, move closer to work

It's not unthinkable. Indeed, this option is increasingly popular, and city planners and developers are growing attuned to what may become a significant trend. Several years ago, John and Robin Mack Davis and their son, Tyler, moved into downtown Greensboro, North Carolina, from the suburbs to live close to the family business, a clothing manufacturing and retail company. Every workday, John and Robin (and their dog, Esme) hoof it three blocks to work. The family has pared down to one low-mileage car, which they use to drive Tyler to school and to go to the grocery store. Their new life in their walkable community "works" for them!

5. Move to a small town

In our book *Moving to a Small Town: A Guidebook for Moving from Urban to Rural America*, Wanda and I chronicled the rising tide of city dwellers opting for rural and small-town living, fueled by new work options like telecommuting and the promise of a simpler, less stressful life. No, small towns and rural communities aren't for everyone, but neither are two hours a day in a car. Sick of the daily commute? Find the small town that fits your needs best and commute five minutes a day!

Time Out, Ref! Time Out!

In the 1938 movie *Holiday*, a stressed-out Cary Grant announces to Katharine Hepburn that he's going to take a "holiday." "To play?" Hepburn asks. "No!" Grant replies. "I want to find out why I'm working. The answer can't just be to pay bills or pile up more money. . . . I can't find out sitting behind some desk in an office. So, as soon as I get enough money together, I'm going to knock off for a while. Come back and work when I know what I'm working for. Does that make sense?"

Why are *you* working? To answer that question, it can help sometimes to take a time-out from your work, as Grant's character does, to reflect on your life as a whole and on your work within the context of that whole. Some of our more progressive companies understand this and find ways to circumvent burnout in their employees by offering leaves of absence, retreats, and other forms of renewal. Taking the long view, savvy employers know from experience that renewal of the human spirit—in the bottom-line language of business—is cost effective.

If it's time for you to follow in Cary Grant's footsteps, consider asking your

Sabbaticals

In their book *Six Months Off*, Hope Dlugozima, James Scott, and David Sharp examine ways to structure a sabbatical. They offer practical advice on how to negotiate time off with your employer. Often, they write, there are others who have taken sabbaticals who work in your company—or who at least work in your industry. Along with these employees who've pioneered a trail, there are typically industry standards pertaining to leaves of absence. Find out what those standards are, then talk to the pioneers. See how they did it, then formulate your plan, taking into account what your financial needs will be during the sabbatical period.

Then make the case to your employer. It helps when the purpose of your sabbatical dovetails with the company's mission and its philosophy about its employees. Will your sabbatical increase your knowledge and skills in a way that will benefit the company? And employers will want to know how you will help the company compensate for the loss of your time.

The perhaps not-so-surprising news is that—not always, of course, but in many instances—when you make a strong case, employers *are* receptive to significant leaves of absence.

If time away is what you need, why not give it your best shot?

employer for serious time off. Maybe it's for that journey to Australia you always wanted to take. Maybe it's to volunteer with a group whose work you admire, or to work on that book you dreamed of writing right out of college. Or maybe it's just to sit in a porch swing and watch the world go by.

The Deathbed Scenario

Here's a scenario for you. You're on your deathbed, your children, spouse, and friends have all gathered round, and someone pipes up, "Well, any regrets, Pops?"

You ponder the question for a moment. And then you say, in your appropriately raspy, deathbed voice, "I have only two."

"Okay, Pops. Tell us. Unburden your soul."

"Fine. My first regret is that I wish I'd worked even more hours at the office."

Someone breaks the stunned silence. "Okay, Pops, so what's number two?"

You draw your next-to-last breath and say, "Number two is that I wish I'd spent all that time at work in a job even *more* meaningless."

Two absurd regrets, at least on their face. But how many of us are living the absurdity of work hours that devour our lives and jobs that alienate us from ourselves? For many of us, the need to "reinvent work," in the phrase of theologian Matthew Fox, is an urgent—perhaps the most urgent—task for the soul, as well as for our physical well-being.

Is this true for you? Do you need to reinvent your work? A good way to answer this question is to listen to your own words. What are you saying to your coworkers about your job? If you aren't expressing yourself directly, what are you saying between the lines? When you're not on the job, what are you telling your family and friends about your work? Observe your own words. What do they reveal to you about your real relationship with the work you do?

"The primary purpose of work," write Thomas H. Naylor, William H. Willimon, and Rolf Osterberg in the book *The Search for Meaning in the Workplace*, "is not to produce goods and services in exchange for paychecks but to serve as a vehicle (one among many others) for the real work we are here to do, to grow as human beings. Further, only work that is in harmony with what we deeply understand as our life purpose is meaningful."

For Quaker author and spiritual leader Rufus Jones, too, knowing why you work is the deepest level of self-knowledge. "We can best discover the principle of the simple life," Jones writes, "by a contrast with the spirit of commercialism. The commercial spirit is selfish. Its motto is 'Expand to get.' . . . Over and against it, at its antipodes, is the spirit of the simple life. It can be lived at any level of poverty or wealth; and at any stage of ignorance or culture. It is essentially the spirit of living for life's sake, or consecration to personal and social goodness. This spirit does not keep us out of commercial business, nor does it command us to confine our business to narrow limits and to small returns. But if we are to belong to the goodly fellowship of those who live the simple life, our business must be made an avenue of ministering to human life."

What *is* the purpose of your life? As we think about work, we must ultimately confront this most difficult of questions. Is your work aligned with what you understand to be your highest calling, your essential self? Do you know your "bliss"— Joseph Campbell's term for "that thing that really gets you deep in your gut, that you feel is your life"?

For many years in my younger days—often years of excruciatingly hard work— I wrestled with these fundamental questions. They led me to conversations with a ghost. That "ghost" was a part of me—another voice, another mind—that seemed to hover in the air close by, a presence invisible yet fully real. That ghost would always say, "But isn't there something *else* you're supposed to be doing with your life? Surely, Frank, old boy, *this* isn't it!"

Do the ghost's queries sound familiar? For me, a sense of purpose in life has come in the gradual realization that my highest "calling"—an old-fashioned term for Campbell's bliss—is that of a teacher. I've realized that, to a large extent, I learn so that I can experience the joy of *teaching* what I learn. Though I've taught many adult classes, I don't teach regularly in a classroom. I teach in an orchard— to pick-your-own customers—about our interconnectedness with nature, about food at its source. I aim to teach as a writer, and at the outdoor Cherry Orchard Theatre I've started. I also want to keep learning as I teach.

Coming from a family saturated with professional teachers, I shouldn't have been surprised by this revelation. Yet, oddly, it was a surprise to me for a time. What I've learned is that it's never too soon—or too late. If you haven't already, why not make every effort now to identify your calling, your bliss?

One simple technique recommended by Campbell himself is to write frequently in a journal about your life and interests, noting where your passions are, what subjects engage you with the greatest frequency and intensity.

Ultimately, what this or some other focused lens for reflection will lead you to is at least the dawning of self-knowledge. From there, your sense of a calling will emerge, as mine did, in much the same way the form of a mountain begins to emerge as fog lifts in the heat of the morning sun.

CHAPTER 4

Lightening Your Footprint

"If you think your actions are too small to make a difference, you've never been in bed with a mosquito."
—Anonymous

You might be single, or you may have a family. You buy just for yourself, or maybe for three or four others. But the point is that your consumption and disposal decisions, your housing and transportation choices, affect only one household, right? No big deal. You take your garbage out every trash day, just like everyone else, to be hauled off to who knows which landfill, where it will decompose by the year 2317—a concept you'd rather not think too deeply about. Certainly, nothing little old you can do could impact something as enormous as the state of the world. After all, what can one person do to turn the tide and lessen the environmental impact of our American lifestyle on Planet Earth? Not much, you say.

Think again. What you can do—starting with nothing's-too-small choices—is to adopt behaviors that acknowledge environmental repercussions and consequences. As these behaviors become automatic in your daily and weekly routines, they will ultimately transform you, your life, your awareness of the world around you, and your feelings about the future. These choices will not only change your life and make you feel like a good guy instead of an environmental bandit, but they will make a difference in the quality of our air, water, soil, landfills, and other measurable indexes. They can help lessen our level of resource use so that we leave a much lighter environmental footprint.

And finally, they will help propel our nation to what Malcolm Gladwell calls "the tipping point"—a place where large-scale environmental change happens, where the conservation and recycling ethic displaces the prevailing ethic favoring consumption, convenience, and disposability over other values. "The best way to understand the emergence of fashion trends . . . ," writes Gladwell in his 2000 bestseller, *The Tipping Point*, "the phenomena of word of mouth, or any number of the other mysterious changes that mark everyday life, is to think of them as epidemics. Ideas and products and messages and behaviors spread just like viruses do."

Your newly chosen behaviors and the message that these changes impart will "spread just like viruses" to the people you influence and to your community. As Gladwell suggests, this is how change happens—at the grass-roots level. Making change is a hand-selling proposition—one person offering a pearl of wisdom to the next, telling a neighbor about a better way to dispose of table scraps, to save gas, to exchange gifts during the holidays.

Multiple and Overlapping Benefits

Each of our life choices—major and minor—can have multiple and overlapping benefits. Thoughtful consumers, in ninety-nine cases out of a hundred, make good environmental stewards. If we gain mastery of our time so that we're making thoughtful choices about how to spend it, we become better environmental stewards. Once you improve your financial planning skills, you're more likely to become a thoughtful consumer, which will tend to curb your purchasing, which in turn will have a positive environmental impact. Choices in one area ripple over to the next.

Once you grasp and adopt the nothing's-too-small principle of environmental stewardship, you can be creative and find little (and big) things in your life that will make a difference. I took up cloth napkins in the early 1990s, having received my first forest-green set as a Christmas gift from my sister Jane. Frank and I have been using cloth instead of paper ever since. We recently learned of a co-housing group of young, single people living in Asheville, North Carolina. The group decided to eliminate paper towels from its pantry and replace them with old-fashioned, washable, reusable rags. A friend of ours saves all the wire hangers and safety pins from her dry cleaning and periodically returns them to the cleaner. Another friend has resolved to never again purchase clothing that needs to be dry-cleaned because of the expense, trouble, and environmental impact of the chemicals used on her garments. "Plus, I hate the plastic wrap that I have to peel off and throw away for each garment," she says. "Each one fills an entire waste can in the bathroom."

Unleash your creativity and dream up more little ideas that you can incorporate in your life to be a better environmental steward.

Big Trouble on a Small Planet

Unless we act now, our children and their children will live in a world of rapidly shrinking horizons. Four major developments—all stemming from everyday human choices—cloud the future like a gathering storm.

First, carbon emissions, methane, and other forms of pollution are trapping solar heat at an unprecedented rate. Without significant reduction, these pollutants are likely to trigger potentially catastrophic—and rapid—climate change.

Second, the combination of a burgeoning global population—there are more than double the number of human beings on the planet as in 1950—and degraded cropland and water sources, if left unchecked, will likely lead to widespread privation and social upheaval.

Third, toxic chemicals—including hazardous waste, pesticides, antifreeze compounds, and many others—pose a looming threat to human health worldwide. Pollution of underground water by petrochemicals, nitrates from fertilizer, and other toxic chemicals is well documented. Contamination from these toxins is suspected to increase the risk of diseases, hormonal abnormalities, and birth defects in human beings and wildlife.

Fourth, life-sustaining ecosystems worldwide are in the path of

The Chairman of the Board

The chairman of the board has his or her prerogatives. He or she runs meetings, calls on speakers, and has the chance to make both sober and heartening announcements.

Recently, in my role as chairman of the board of the Greater Mount Airy Chamber of Commerce, I decided to make a point of bringing my travel mug to our meetings. Most months, I just brought mine in without comment, but once or twice, I recognized board members who did the same and challenged others to follow suit. My dear friend Ann Vaughn began carrying in her travel mug for each meeting. Ann's nephew, Rick Vaughn, started doing the same. By the end of my one-year term, by no means was the entire board bringing in travel mugs on the second Tuesday at eight in the morning at the local Hampton Inn, but the idea had been planted in their minds that it might just be a good thing to do.

What I learned from this experience is to never assume that a group is not receptive to your ideas. The business community, for instance, has probably never been more receptive to the call for environmental stewardship. If you state your case in a positive, upbeat manner, you never know how many lives you will influence.

the ravenous beast of human culture, with its grave threats to tropical forests and global forest cover generally, wetlands, coral reefs, and other ecosystems. Extinction of species continues unabated, the consequences of which are largely unforeseeable. Half of all the earth's animal and plant species live in rain forests, unique ecosystems being destroyed at the rate of fifty acres per minute.

Why Denial and Disconnect?

In the face of such large, potentially apocalyptic threats, the easiest course is to bury our heads in the sand. Denial is a powerful human instinct; passengers on the *Titanic*, it's safe to say, were not disposed to embrace the end game of hitting that iceberg until the ship started its deadly plunge into the frigid waters and panic ensued. And because we don't normally *see* the damage that is the result of our lifestyle choices—don't see forests decimated, or carbon emissions trapping heat—we live in a perpetual state of disconnect, not viscerally connecting the dots between our personal behaviors and ecological calamity.

Residual Guilt: The First Hurdle

The first hurdle to overcome on the path to change is ridding ourselves of the collective sense of guilt that we feel about the state of the planet. Whether or not we admit it, whether we identify ourselves as environmentalists or prefer to dismiss these concerns as "alarmist," most Americans carry a nagging sense of guilt about our roles in the despoiling of the environment.

"We're all in it," our friend Nick Bragg once remarked, meaning that virtually no one living in North America is exempt from leaving environmental damage in his or her wake. Guilt is not a pretty emotion; it's paralyzing, rather than empowering. But making nothing's-too-small choices can start you on a path to change, can help you regain your sense that the world is a good place with a promising future.

So how can saving paper clips, picking up aluminum cans, washing and reusing baggies, bundling your errands so you drive less frequently, buying used clothing, and turning your thermostat up in the summer and down in the winter affect the pending environmental catastrophe we describe?

"Every act of consumption has an environmental impact," says Gary Gardner, head of research for the Worldwatch Institute in Washington, D.C. "If there's material or energy being used, there's an environmental impact." In the past, many environmental advocacy groups focused on how government and big business could address environmental concerns. But increasingly, groups like Worldwatch are addressing how individual consumption choices—especially in America and the First World—impact the environment. These groups are focusing on how to prepare the population for widespread change. What is called for is a paradigm shift, and with it major behavioral change.

Finding Your Own "Click" Moment

The smallest change is never, in fact, too small. For me, a "click" moment came one day at work in the early 1980s in a city where angels are rumored to hover in the smog. At my desk at the *Los Angeles Herald-Examiner*, I sipped the dregs of yet another cup of coffee in yet another Styrofoam cup and tossed the one-use-only cup into the trash can. *Click.* Forgetting my deadline, I stared at a freeze-frame avalanche of discarded white cups, each used once and thrown away, each ticketed for the landfill.

I stared. And my life changed.

I purchased a travel mug. For the remainder of my time in Los Angeles, and later in my new home in the South, I carried that travel mug everywhere I went—in the car, on trips, to my office, to board meetings, even to church on Sunday.

What difference did that make? Well, by a conservative estimate, figuring that

I would have used just *one* Styrofoam cup a day, over a twenty-year period, I would have spared seventy-two hundred Styrofoam cups that dreary trek to the landfill. "Nothing's too small," I told family and friends, "to make a difference." Not even one Styrofoam cup.

Nothing is indeed too small, especially when you consider the power of numbers, that warm and fuzzy phenomenon of people influencing people, friends talking to friends, people modeling their behavior from what they see of others. Think about it: If just one person duplicated my travel-mug conversion, over twenty years, that would collectively account for keeping nearly fifteen thousand Styrofoam cups out of a landfill. If three more followed suit, over twenty years' time, that would save an additional twenty-two thousand Styrofoam cups. Suddenly, the power of one becomes the power of many, a mighty force that can help turn the tide.

If you're like Frank and me, you get a nagging feeling inside you each time you fill a garbage bag with the throw-away detritus from an office party or a child's

---

The Greening of the Office

At Worldwatch headquarters just off Dupont Circle in Washington, D.C., office staffers attempt to live consistently with their values and to minimize their environmental footprints. Try taking a page out of Worldwatch's book—we do the same here at our office in Mount Airy—by adopting many of these practices to "green" your own office:

* *Bring your own mug.* Invite each employee to bring in a favorite ceramic mug for coffee, tea, and other beverages.

* *Contribute guest mugs.* Ask employees if there are any ceramic mugs at home that they'd like to contribute to the guest-mug supply. Then be sure you have a goodly number of these floater mugs for visitors, so you won't have to resort to throwaways when they come in.

* *Organize a "Greening of the Office Committee"* to make primary decisions about how to "green" your office. These decisions may include what temperature you want to leave the thermostat on, whether you'd like employees to bring in cut flowers or potted plants, and how you want to clean the office.

* *Save coffee grounds for compost.* You can use a plastic bag in the freezer or a tin coffee can with a plastic lid. Offer them to anyone who gardens at home.

* *Try tea towels.* A tea towel is an Australian name for a dish towel, which is used to dry coffee cups, plates, glasses, and cutlery. Rotate weeks on

birthday celebration, and when you purchase something that you might already own but don't want to take the time to look for (since you have no earthly idea where it is), and when you speed back to the grocery store for a gallon of milk, having already made the same trip twice before that day. You may not realize it, but part of what ails you is the sense that you are not being a good environmental steward.

So listen to the voice inside you and find your own environmental "click" moment. You may resolve to eat fewer (or no more) frozen dinners, or to never again patronize a fast-food chain because of the mountain of disposables that lies in the wake of a single meal. Or you may decide to never again give a gift just for the sake of giving a gift, or to give gifts only to people who really need or want them. "Never again will I give a 'make-gift,' " a friend recently commented. (A "make-gift" is the equivalent of "make-work"; it's a gift neither needed nor wanted.)

Here's a strategy that works. If you make a resolution—like I did with my

---

who gets to take them home to launder.

* *Substitute cloth towels for paper towels.* At the Simple Living office, we have both available, but we now replace our paper-towel roll just once a month or every six weeks, rather than once a week. Most of our customers simply prefer cloth towels. Just make sure you keep them laundered.

* *Stock your refrigerator.* A well-stocked refrigerator uses less energy than a sparsely stocked one. If necessary, fill the space with water in gallon jugs as needed. This concept applies to freezers as well.

* *Bring in goodies.* Anytime one of us in the office feels celebratory, we bring in food to share—such as Laura's famous home-baked brownies or lemon squares. During fruit season, Frank and I bring in cherries, peaches, or apples to have on hand. There's nothing like breaking bread to bring us together in common purpose.

* *Rotate kitchen cleanup.* Nothing is as much of a turnoff as a dirty common kitchen. Create a sign-up sheet so that kitchen cleanup is rotated.

* *Recycle paper.* At the Simple Living office, we always reuse white paper, except for confidential memos and financial information, which we shred and recycle. As a result of our practice, many memos are printed out on the backside of Henry's lesser artwork, old chamber-of-commerce memos, and even the yellowing first draft of my mother's 1971 Ph.D. dissertation on Margaret Fuller.

travel mug—don't beat yourself up for backsliding occasionally. If you do that, you're likely to abandon your resolve altogether. Sure, in the twenty years since I officially swore off Styrofoam cups, beverages in Styrofoam have occasionally met my lips. But by and large, I have held to my pledge.

Recycling for Fun and College

When we resolved in the late 1980s to simplify our lives, one of the first practices we adopted was recycling. Since there was no curbside recycling pickup program in rural Carroll County, Virginia, we had to set up our own recycling center at home. We did this in the landing to the basement in our orchard home, using wooden, bushel-sized apple crates. Into these we sorted different colors of glass, aluminum, steel cans, and plastics. The beauty of the system is that we can stack box upon box—almost indefinitely, it seems—before having to take a trip to the recycling center at the Carroll County Sanitary Landfill in Hillsville.

Another fun outing we make around recycling is to drop by David Pearce's Mount Airy Iron & Metal business, down by the railroad tracks in Mount Airy. Frank and I and our six-year-old son, Henry, load up the orchard's pickup truck with crates filled with Henry's favorite: the aluminum cans that seem to proliferate at every turn. We collect them at the Levering Orchard pack house and our outdoor orchard theater in summer and fall and at our office in downtown Mount Airy year-round. For those aluminum cans, Henry earns a little money for his college fund, and we have the satisfaction of knowing all the goodies we bring David will bypass that trip to the landfill and see a new incarnation. Henry likes reciting a fact that his aunt Jane passed on to us: "Did you know that the energy saved in recycling *one* aluminum can will run your television set for *three* hours?" Running a television set for three whole hours—especially when Disney cartoon classics like *Dumbo, The Fox and the Hound,* and *Alice in Wonderland* are on—is a delightful prospect for Henry, not unlike the fantasy of having an entire cake to himself and not having to share a piece.

David Pearce is a gentle soul, a tall, soft-spoken man who tousles Henry's hair as he hands our bright-eyed lad his money. On a recent trip, smashed and flattened aluminum cans weighing a total of six pounds earned two dollars for Henry's college fund.

"Still picking up cans?" David teased me about my locally famous custom of halting when strolling down the street to pick up an aluminum can and stow it in a plastic crate in the back of my station wagon. Its destination is back home in an apple crate. This has become a regular habit of mine. And I've grown more aggressive in practicing it than I was in the early 1990s, when I did it on the sly when no one was looking, so as to avoid being mistaken for a bag lady or being thought eccentric. Now, when I stroll the streets of Mount Airy, I pick up these cans and occasional pieces of trash to help keep the downtown of this place I love litter free.

The Big Three: "Speed, Feed, and Heat"

On a recent trip to Washington, D.C., Frank and I had a chance to visit the headquarters of the Worldwatch Institute, respected internationally as perhaps the world's leading research outfit on global environmental issues. Since 1984, as part of its mission to promote a sustainable society globally, Worldwatch has issued annual interdisciplinary reports under the title *State of the World*. Frank's father, Sam, always alert to global issues, used to purchase these books by the box load and hand them out to friends with memorable zest and urgency.

The director of research at Worldwatch, Gary Gardner, a soft-spoken man who often bikes to work from his Alexandria, Virginia, home, presides over a humming hive of incoming data and thoroughgoing analysis. Over the years, Gary has written extensively on environmental issues, most recently an overview of human consumption's impact on the environment.

We talked with Gary in his office. On a second trip, I visited him and his family at home. I asked Gary what Americans can do in our everyday lives to make a positive difference toward the environment.

The three critical areas on which we should focus, he said, are "speed, feed, and heat." He cited a recent report by the Union of Concerned Scientists. This report, Gary said, suggests that Americans can have the greatest positive impact by focusing on "the way we transport ourselves, the way we eat, . . . and the way we heat and cool our homes."

Buy Aluminum

When you're faced with a beverage-buying decision in the supermarket or at a gas station, always opt for aluminum cans over plastic or glass—and certainly over those dreadful, overly packaged juice boxes that are so popular with kids. The reason? Aluminum is the easiest item to recycle. If you recycle nothing else, recycle aluminum. The market is active and thriving. You can make money from aluminum. And if you're not interested in the small change it generates, any civic or church group will be happy to take it off your hands. (In my church, there is a freestanding box for aluminum cans, ready to accept them anytime.) In addition, aluminum cans are so light that you can easily carry a small plastic crate of them in the back without weighing down your car. What's more, they're easy to crush.

Speed

If you want to start with one of Gary Gardner's Big Three, why not choose transportation? How do you, in your daily life, get from one place to another? Do you drive a car, truck, or SUV? Most of us do. As of late 2003, United States households had an average of 1.9 cars, trucks, and sport utility vehicles—about one-fourth of the world's private vehicle fleet. According to Worldwatch, American cars and light trucks "account for 40 percent of the nation's oil use and contribute about as much to climate change as all economic activity in Japan does." What can we do to lessen our negative impact on the environment, particularly the amount of carbon emissions our vehicles generate when we drive?

In all good conscience, we *must* do something. And keep in mind the multiple and overlapping benefits of nothing's-too-small choices. For example, to drive the speed limit, you need to give yourself that cushion of time we talked about in chapter 1, so that you're not constantly running late.

Here are ten basic strategies:

1. As we suggested in chapter 3, if feasible, move closer to where you work, so as to decrease your travel time. Urban sprawl, which has planted many of us in the suburbs far from our workplaces, has taken a toll on the environment. Consider a relocation that would cause less wear and tear not only on the environment but also on you!

2. Arrange to telecommute on your job so that you have no commute at all.

3. If you can't telecommute every day, try doing so every other day, twice a week, twice a month—whenever you can.

4. If you're in the new or used car market, consider buying the most fuel-efficient vehicle you can use and afford. If a hybrid isn't what you need, consider a passenger car rather than an SUV. If you need a big-capacity vehicle, why not select a more fuel-efficient van than an SUV? SUV's currently emit twice as much carbon dioxide per mile as typical cars, and they spew up to five and a half times the quantity of smog-causing gases. Ford Motors chairman William Ford has apologized for making SUV's, calling his Excursion "the Ford Valdez" for its pollution-spilling qualities. Remarkably, he condemned SUV's as wasteful and polluting but declared that his company would continue to manufacture them because they are profitable. Quite simply—particularly if you live in an urban or suburban

environment—ask yourself why your "need" for an SUV outweighs the damages incurred.

5. Whenever possible, carpool. In urban areas, this brings the advantage of allowing you to use HOV lanes on freeways. When you carpool, you're also building community and enjoying fellowship as you go.

6. Observe the speed limit. This saves gas and helps save your sanity. And it might just save your life.

7. Give your vehicle regular tune-ups to ensure maximum fuel efficiency.

8. Lighten the load in your vehicle. Check to make sure you're not hauling around unnecessary heavy boxes or items. If you rarely use a car seat or find yourself hauling around a toolbox loaded with hammers, wrenches, and power tools, remove these extraneous items and bring them back for occasions when you know you'll be needing them.

9. Check the air pressure in your tires at least once a month. Properly inflated tires promote fuel efficiency.

10. When shopping or running errands, bundle your errands so you're not constantly making new trips.

Consider a Car Share

If you live in a city that has car-share services, check them out. The new Zip Car service in Washington, D.C., and the City Car Share program in San Francisco, for example, offer consumers affordable twenty-four-hour access to private vehicles for short-term, round-trip use. It's an efficient complement to public transportation. Once customers join the service, they sell their old cars and avoid buying new ones. Older, less fuel-efficient vehicles are replaced with newer ones, which have more stringent controls. Fewer parking spaces are needed, thus preserving green space. According to Worldwatch, car sharing still represents a small percentage of vehicle miles traveled worldwide, but the concept is experiencing explosive growth.

And Now, the Fun (Speed) Stuff

There's always walking, of course (see chapter 7). It's great exercise and emits no carbon dioxide! You are one of a very small and privileged minority if you're able to walk to work—only about 2 percent of North Carolinians do. More than one-quarter of Americans' automobile trips amount to a mile or less, and 14 percent of our trips are less than half a mile. Why not—at least some of the time—walk?

Nor should we neglect motorcycles. I can't claim to be a motorcyclist, but our friend Dick Hanratty swears by the one he rides near his Bremerton, Washington, home. They cause less pollution and are more fun.

And what about that staple of many a college campus and many a city in other parts of the world—the bicycle? Are bikes a realistic alternative to motor-driven vehicles?

Ask actor and environmentalist Ed Begley, Jr., whom Frank and I visited recently at his Studio City, California, home, and the answer is a resounding yes. A tall, handsome, athletic man whose many credits include the television series *St. Elsewhere* and whose environmental roots stretch back to the original Earth Day in 1970, Ed lives in an urban environment seemingly as hostile to bicycles as one could imagine. Frank and I know Ed's cityscape well. Our own six years as a Los Angeles couple commenced with Frank's driving a cab for the Red Top Taxi Company and my commuting to work on the Santa Monica Freeway. Somehow, in that world of asphalt and sprawl, Ed's 1980s-vintage bike is, as he told us, "my number one form of transportation."

Ed's quest to find alternatives to King Oil goes back to 1970 as well—the year he bought his first electric car, for $950. Today, the family garage at the home of Ed, his wife, Rachelle, and their young daughter, Hayden, houses Ed's bike, his current electric car, and a hybrid car driven primarily by his wife. The three "speed" alternatives give the family a range of options that, for Ed, always begins with his bicycle.

"I bike somewhere every day," he told us. "I ride to get where I'm going. Riding a bicycle is good for the environment, good for your health, and good for traffic and less dependence on foreign oil. . . . Many times, I've pulled up to a film or television location on a bicycle. I live in Studio City, and we were shooting in a town called Fillmore, and it's about maybe sixty, sixty-five miles away, and I rode there on my bicycle. I'll ride anywhere on my bike. I can get to Santa Monica in an hour and ten minutes, and you know, the truth is, in rush-hour traffic, you're not going to do much better than that. And I get there invigorated, I've got my endorphin rush, I've got a change of clothes in my backpack, and I go freshen up somewhere in a restroom, and I'm ready to go! It's a good bike, and the beautiful thing is, it's also a mountain bike. So you can ride it on the road or ride it on trails. So I can go over these trails and get to Beverly Hills and not encounter one car— beautiful trails with rabbits running in the path, and occasionally you see some deer. That's my version of a morning commute—and a darn good one!"

Much as we would have liked to, Frank and I didn't get a chance to ride in Ed's electric car. But we watched him drive it into his garage and "refuel" it from the charger on the wall. "You just open the little flap on the car like a gas tank," Ed explained, demonstrating, "only it's electrons, not fuel." Inserting the nozzlelike attachment from the charger, Ed told us, "If you're fully depleted, it takes a few hours to recharge, but usually I'm half-depleted or so, so in about an hour, you're topped off again. So you can come home and shower and get ready to go out for the evening, and you've got a full tank again if you need to drive a long way."

A "long way," for Ed's electric car, cannot exceed eighty miles without charging. But that's not a problem, Ed told us. "To Hollywood and back, that round trip is fourteen miles. To Beverly Hills and back is sixteen miles. To LAX from here is eighteen miles. I've never had an appointment in L.A. that I couldn't make in an electric car."

Ed's other mode of getting around in L.A. is public transportation, a system that has improved markedly since Frank and I lived there in the 1980s. Americans use public transportation for only 2 percent of all urban trips. Compare this with a century ago, when the United States led all nations in public transit ridership. If only we could follow Ed's lead! I had a chance to ride with Ed on a public bus we boarded on Ventura Boulevard just two blocks from his house. Ed told me he takes the bus "a couple times a week. Taking it downtown is a no-brainer. It costs ninety cents for a token, and you can't park downtown for ninety cents. I take it downtown or to Hollywood all the time. It's a natural-gas bus, so it's very clean. So it's good for the environment and good for cutting down on traffic congestion. Besides, on a bus, you get to read, relax, and meditate. You can't do much of that on the 405 [freeway]."

Since Frank and I lived in town, Los Angeles has developed a subway system that Ed also uses occasionally. "It goes from the [San Fernando] valley, where I live, all the way to downtown, to Union Station. There is also a blue line that goes all the way south to Long Beach, and a green line that goes to El Segundo and points east. It's a great system!"

Ed's enthusiasm for—and commitment to—alternative transportation in the heart of the car capital of the United States is quite a story. Perhaps it will inspire you, as it did Frank and me. For the time being, our own two gas-powered six- and ten-year-old cars with their five-speed manual transmissions, modest engines, and relatively good fuel efficiency—Frank's Geo Prizm gets thirty-nine miles per gallon—suit us. But we hope that as prices fall and advances continue on hybrid models and other new technologies, you, too, will consider these alternatives—while not forgetting the old-fashioned virtues of bicycling! If, like Ed Begley, Jr., you have an environmental conscience, you're sure to get a better night's sleep!

Car Envy: The Hybrid from Heaven

"Green machines," a recent article in Sierra magazine called them. They're the vehicles that challenge the drill-and-drive vision of the automotive experience. In a world where, by 2020, it's estimated there will be nearly 1.5 billion cars, green machines offer hope for less polluted air and at least a partial reversal of the trend toward global warming. The still-evolving green machines run on natural gas and ethanol, on electricity, on fuel cells, on a combination of hydrogen and oxygen—even, in the central North Carolina town of Misenheimer, a hub for "bio fuels," on old kitchen grease or used vegetable oil. The twenty or so such vehicles in the Misenheimer area are called "grease-cars." Is there one in your future?

For hybrid cars—vehicles with gas-powered engines that collaborate with electric motors for fuel economy—the future is now. It was in Charlotte that I test-drove my first hybrid, an increasingly popular choice among environmentally conscious drivers. It's an experience I'd love to have every day.

Back in 2001, Lisa Renstrom bought what she believes was the first hybrid car in the Charlotte market. "My husband keeps up on cars, and he said, 'You've got to go look at this car,' " Lisa told me outside her Charlotte home. The two-door, two-seat Honda Insight was still up on lifts at the dealership when she first spotted it. Though the salesman knew nothing about it, he faked it and said, "This is probably going to go quick!"

Salesman's hype aside, Lisa took one look at the silver, bullet-shaped beauty and fell in love. She put down three hundred dollars on the car, came back the next week to test-drive it, and hasn't looked back since. "It's like any other car, except that you get this fabulous gas mileage," she said. "It's an ultra-low-emissions vehicle. . . . Under current technology, this is the best emission you can get."

"So it lessens your environmental footprint," I said.

"Absolutely! That's why I bought the car."

I have to admit being overcome by a sudden and unexpected case of car envy. And when Lisa related how much less time she spends at the gas pump, the pangs intensified. "I hate going to the gas station," she said. With her Insight, she has to make the trip little more than once a month. She puts twelve thousand miles on her Insight annually and figures that, at current prices, she saves five hundred dollars a year on gas.

A Moving Report Card

On the car's dashboard is a monitor that offers continuous feedback about gas mileage—a kind of moving report card. "It tells you all the time while you're driving what mileage you're getting." This challenges Lisa and her husband to think about how efficiently they're driving. "My husband likes to use it competitively," Lisa laughed, "because he likes to see that he can get better gas mileage than I do."

The car, a stick shift, generally gets about sixty miles per gallon in the city and seventy on the highway. Her husband drives a high-performance Porsche Carrera, the car they use for nights on the town and long trips. But Lisa finds her hybrid perfect for grocery shopping, runs to the airport, and errands in town.

One fringe benefit Lisa enjoys is feeling like a kind of knight in shining environmental armor riding around Charlotte in her sporty little buggy. Especially in its first year in Lisa's hands—before there were many hybrids on the road—people would stop her in parking lots and ask, "What *is* that?"

"I'd explain, and they were incredulous," Lisa said. "They were very supportive." On the road, she said, "people would give me the thumbs-up when they saw it."

When I test-drove Lisa's car, I especially liked it that the engine cut off when the car came to a halt (another means of saving gas) and then seamlessly restarted. However, despite the new-car lust I temporarily felt in my heart, I came back home to my Subaru wagon and reaffirmed my commitment. "I love this car," I told myself, "especially because it's paid for." Though the Subaru is reasonably fuel efficient, I did resolve that if the need for a new car ever arises, I will definitely give a hybrid strong consideration.

Planes, Trains, and Such

A brief word to the wise: As much as possible, let air travel be for the birds. Worldwide, according to Worldwatch Institute, "only 0.5 percent of the total distance people travel each year is done by air, yet planes use up about 5 percent of transportation energy." While it's not always practical to avoid airplane travel, it's worth remembering that each plane trip you make carries a steep environmental price tag. Consider other forms of transportation whenever possible, particularly if your automobile is fuel efficient. And consider taking the train. Compared to automobiles, trains burn half the fuel per passenger mile.

Feed

If Gary Gardner is right, "feed"—the food we eat, and how it gets to our table—is very much "on the table" as an environmental issue. In the chapter "Watching What We Eat" in the *State of the World* 2004 report, authors Brian Halweil and Danielle Nierenberg observe, "Our food choices rival transportation as the human activity with the greatest impact on the environment. One

> ### Conserve Water
>
> To conserve water when you flush, install an ultralow-flow toilet. And for that shower, twenty bucks or so will buy you a high-efficiency shower head.

European study found that food consumption accounts for between 10 and 20 percent of the environmental impact of the average household. When Annika Carlson-Kanyama at the University of Stockholm compared the amount of greenhouse gas emissions generated by different food choices, she found that a meat-rich meal made with imported ingredients emits nine times as much carbon as a vegetarian meal made with domestically produced ingredients that do not have to be hauled long distances."

To many of us, the magnitude of food's environmental impact may come as a surprise. More than, say, the carbon emissions from our automobiles, food tends to fly under our "environmental radar," except as a health issue.

As we make our food choices, there are many factors to consider in both senses of the word *environment*. Our choices link personal health with global environmental health. For this reason, we have chosen to write about food and health at length in chapter 7. There, you will find a detailed menu of choices to make about food—

choices good for the environment and good for you, too!

Heat

Regarding the word *heat*, Gary Gardner's useful mnemonic device for environmental stewardship really applies to all the energy and other environmentally sensitive choices we make in our home environment—how we both heat and cool our homes, what materials we use in home construction, how much electricity we use. You *can* make a difference in your home. Here are some things to look at:

1. Consider a smaller living space when you're buying or building a house

Granted, you'll be bucking the current American trend. Despite the fact that nearly a quarter of the earth's population has either poor shelter or no shelter at all, square footage in new homes in the United States grew 38 percent between 1975 and 2000. Typically, with bigger living spaces comes increased energy use. There's more space to cool, heat, and light, as well as more and larger appliances. Refrigerators, for example, increased in average size by 10 percent during that same period.

Arguably, in addition to the environmental price tag of larger living spaces, there's a psychic price as well. Excessively large living spaces scatter family members in their own homes. And as architect Sarah Susanka, author of *The Not So Big House*, observes, "Many of the huge rooms we see in magazines today are really only comfortable when they are filled with people. For one or two, or for a family, they can be overwhelming. And when rooms feel overwhelming, they don't get used."

The home of Ed Begley, Jr., in Studio City tells a very different story. Following his financial success as a Hollywood actor, Ed told us, friends and people "in the business" suggested that he move from his modest, seventeen-hundred-square-foot house to a super-sized home more suitable to an actor of his stature. Ed wouldn't budge. With solar panels he'd installed on his roof in 1989 providing energy, and with a living space on a human scale, Ed stayed the course. He now lives cozily with his wife and young daughter in charming digs that are modest only by American standards. Homes in Europe and Japan, for example, average about eleven hundred square feet. In Africa, the average is less than a hundred square feet.

Not-so-big houses require us, in Sarah Susanka's words, "to think creatively, responding to needs and wishes, not to preconceived notions of what a house should be." Interior designer DD Allen says of smaller spaces with which she's worked, "What I like about my places is that when you're there with people, it really forces you to be engaged. I appreciate intimacy, and I find a lot of people who live in big places feel comfortable in my small ones."

For the environment and for your psyche, if you're building or buying a house, think not-so-big. Live on a human scale.

2. Examine your heating, cooling, and water-heating systems

These are the three biggest energy drains on the home front. A few "small" things can pay big dividends.

First, turn your thermostat down (or up) by at least three degrees. The energy you save will more than compensate for the short period of acclimatization you'll experience. And don't turn the thermostat on and off. It's more energy efficient to maintain a set temperature in your home than to frequently switch the thermostat.

Second, consider ceiling fans as an alternative to air conditioning, especially in regions of the country rarely stricken by high heat and

---

"Stuff-lock"

What happens when we buy and possess a lot of stuff?
Essentially, three things.

First, we clutter our living space. Or if we can't stand the clutter, we store a lot of stuff elsewhere. Every year, Americans rent a billion square feet of storage space in which to store stuff we may—or may not—use someday.

Second, we spend a lot of time and energy dealing with all that stuff. Often, this leads to "stuff-lock"—the feeling of being overwhelmed by one's own stuff. Richard Swenson, a physician and author of *The Overload Syndrome*, calls this "possession overload." It's the feeling, Swenson says, that "everything I own owns me. People feel sad and what do they do? They go to the mall and shop and it makes them feel better, but only for a short time. There's an addictive quality in consumerism."

Third, by buying and (perhaps) using a lot of stuff, we impact the environment. Each purchase we make has an environmental story, often hidden from our view, and not always happy. Consider, as one example, the purchase of a computer. In their book *Affluenza*, John de Graaf, David Wann, and Thomas H. Naylor tell the environmental story behind one purchase. "When we buy a computer," they write, "it doesn't occur to us that 700 or more different materials went into it, converging from mines, oil derricks, and chemical factories all over the world. The sleek, colorful machine purring on each desktop generated 140 pounds of solid and hazardous waste in its manufacture, along with 7,000 gallons of wastewater, and about a humidity. In our home, we've found that ceiling fans work very well, even when the temperature outdoors is in the mid-eighties or even hotter.

Third, especially if it's an older house, make sure it's well insulated. Weather-strip, seal, and caulk your doors, windows, and pipes. Every crack and gap sucks out energy.

Fourth, consider replacing an old water heater, washer, dryer, dishwasher, or other appliance with a more energy-efficient model.

3. When building, consider your house's orientation

Dan Chiras, an author and consultant on solar energy, says that, by building your home facing south, "you're going to have a 10 percent lower annual fuel bill for heating and cooling because the house will be warmer in winter and cooler in the summer. And if you just move a few windows to that south side, you can reduce your cooling and heating bills by up to 30 percent."

---

fourth of its lifetime energy consumption. Every year, more than twelve million computers—amounting to more than 300,000 tons of electronic junk—are disposed of. The point is, when we buy a computer, all the rest comes with it, even if it's *out of sight, out of mind.*"

Waste. Pollution. Energy consumption. Resource depletion. In addition to the economic story—the money spent, the income generated in the economies participating in the manufacture and sale of that computer—there's the story of an endangered planet. That's the real cost of an item.

Stuff-lock, then, is more than the feeling of being overwhelmed by one's own stuff. It's the feeling that our consumption habits are ravaging the environment. That, too, can lead to a feeling of being overwhelmed, a kind of paralysis in which we believe there's nothing we can do to reverse environmental degradation. After all, that computer we just purchased, we have to have it, don't we? We have no other choice.

In fact, we *must* make another choice. As Alan Durning, coauthor of *Stuff: The Secret Lives of Everyday Things*, tells us, that choice is "about creating a lifestyle that doesn't require as much stuff to make us even happier than we are now." It's about thoughtful consumption. In making thoughtful purchases, we do the homework that tells us the environmental story of those purchases. We weigh the hidden costs of an item before we buy it—costs that are hidden only because we don't live where we can see and experience, directly and for ourselves, the environmental impact.

And we pass on our knowledge. It's one boat, after all, that we're all in together. Knowledge is power. Both in our purchases and in our influence on others, our knowledge is not too small to make a difference.

4. Plant energy-saving vegetation near your home

For example, if you need cooling shade for the sunny side of your house, think Bradford pear trees. These fast-growing, attractive deciduous trees provide plenty of leafy protection in the summer but don't screen the sun in winter.

Sweat the Small (Electrical) Stuff

The use of electricity translates directly into greenhouse-gas emissions. That's the bottom line to remember on the "small" electricity-users in our living spaces—not only household appliances, but also computers (Americans burn 2 percent of our electricity using computers and the Internet alone), televisions, and light bulbs.

Light bulbs? You bet. All told, lighting accounts for 34 percent of American electricity use, yet those lights burning in our homes can easily be dismissed as of little consequence. As with all things electrical, turn them off if you don't need them! It makes a difference. And instead of those same old incandescent bulbs, install compact fluorescent bulbs, which use one-fourth the energy of standard incandescent bulbs and last ten times longer.

Reduce Your Personal Waste Stream

Roughly one-third of all the waste that goes into landfills is rotable organic waste—that is, yard clippings and food waste that emit the greenhouse gas methane. Methane is an environmental culprit that has not gotten the press of carbon dioxide. "Molecule per molecule, methane is much more powerful, in terms of its potential to warm the planet, than carbon dioxide," says Gary Gardner. "So every time we throw an organic product away, we are running the potential of creating more methane emissions." Instead of tossing your banana peels into the trash bag alongside nonrecyclable plastic waste, Styrofoam, and other matter, why not take matters into your own hands and invite some worms into your home?

Wormy Business

One practice that Gary Gardner and his wife, Sally, have adopted to reduce their personal waste stream is putting a worm bin in the basement of their modest Alexandria, Virginia, home. This is something you can do in a small home or even an apartment. All you need is a bin and some worms to get started. A ten-gallon

Going Green on Cape Cod

It had been a long time, but there Frank and I were again, out on wind-swept Cape Cod on a cold December day much like the one nearly twenty years before when we'd attended an after-Christmas family wedding. It wasn't matrimony that brought us back; it was an invitation from Matt Miller of Miller Boehm Architects in Boston to tour a just-completed "green" house designed by his firm.

And what exactly is a green house? "A green house is a sustainably designed house, which means that it is designed with extra consciousness toward the environment, toward using natural materials and being more energy efficient, and also creating a more comfortable environment for the inhabitants," said architect Miller.

Which means what? The "comfortable environment" we could plainly see and feel—a warm, two-story space that was "simple and understated," as Miller described it. But what was harder to see were the green ingredients. The insulation, for example. Miller's firm had specified that the blown-in foam insulation that completely fills the cavities in the extra-thick walls contain no CFCs or other harmful chemicals.

Now, here was a design that was serious about energy efficiency. "A good, comfortable envelope is very important," Miller told us. So, along with thick walls and dense insulation, the exterior of the house boasts what he described as "a thin skin of insulating board" that "covers over all the parts of the house." Additionally, it has "bits of wood that create thermal bridges and allow the heat to transfer out of the house. This creates an extra protective blanket."

Miller wasn't finished with us. His design also utilizes what he called "rain-screen technology," which creates a drainage plane immediately outside the house. This small, one-inch air pocket prevents moisture from accumulating and thus waterproofs the house. The finishing materials—such as the ubiquitous shingles—are held out from the drainage plane so that air can pass behind them. This air flow keeps the shingles dry and prevents moisture and mildew damage.

Then there are the house's double-paned "tilt-turn" windows, which tilt inward slightly to allow continuous ventilation. The windows' sashes have a "sophisticated gasketing system," Miller explained, "which keeps cold air out and reduces heat loss."

This house is built to last. Miller told us it should survive a hundred years, in sharp contrast to the twenty- to forty-year span usually anticipated these days in new-home construction. Longevity in itself is a green attribute—a more efficient use of resources. And it's better food for the soul. As architect Sarah Susanka writes, "We are slowly coming to understand that if we build for our short-term needs alone, with buildings that self-destruct in only a generation or two, there will be no sense of past and no sense of soul."

bin or plastic storage container should handle the waste of two people. If you live alone, a five-gallon bucket will likely do the job. Then you'll need to buy some worms. Generally, the so-called red wrigglers found in bait shops work best. Or you can contact WormDigest.org, which provides links to worm growers and offers online chat sessions about worm composting and vermi-composting.

You'll need to keep your worm bin well ventilated with small holes at the top and bottom of the bin, covered by screen. And be sure to place a tray beneath the bin to catch any leakage, which makes an excellent "worm tea," an outstanding, nutritious supplement for houseplants.

To start a bed, fill your bin with a foot of wet bedding such as yard waste, plant clippings, or even newsprint, then add a layer of soil. Place your bin where the temperature hovers between sixty and seventy-five degrees. The best foods for the worms are vegetable and fruit waste, plant and yard waste, coffee grounds (including filters), eggshells, and the like. After the worms have had a chance to do their magic, you'll be left with rich topsoil that is great for either the garden or houseplants.

Set Forth

Deciding to lighten your environmental footprint need not be an odious task. In fact, once you get started, it can be downright fun. It is guaranteed to lift your spirits and let you soar. If you decide to incorporate nothing's-too-small steps into your life, you'll have the potential to change your life.

As we read testimonials from people who have blazed their own paths to simpler living, who have determined to make changes large and small to improve their lives, we've been reinforced in our conviction to carry on this work and to inspire others to do the same. As with all nothing's-too-small choices, the magic moment comes when you simply decide to act. Instead of being paralyzed by inaction or frozen in place by the gravity of the problem before you, take one small step. It will be a step toward a glorious future.

CHAPTER 5

Teach Your Children Well

"We must all work to make the world worthy of its children."

—Pablo Casals

As much as simple living has the potential to transform your life as an adult, setting the stage for simplicity in your child's life is arguably more important. Why? Because young people—from babies to children to teens to young adults—represent the future. And because giving impressionable young people a grounding in the fundamentals of simplicity is one of the most significant foundational legacies anyone can bequeath.

Never has it been more challenging to do this than today. All Americans are swimming against a riptide of consumerism, commercialism, and depersonalizing technology, but for parents, the swim is arguably the hardest. With all the contradictory messages we parents receive (compounded by strong input from our children), it's easy to get confused and lose our way. So many of us believe that we're doing right by our children by working overtime to pay for "advantages" meant to set the stage for promising futures for our youngsters. It often takes two high-powered careers to be able to afford to live in the right school district, to buy our kids the latest clothes, to feed them, to pay for health care, to cover the extras. And all too often, driving our children as we do ourselves, we push them to achieve in school and sign them up for so many extracurricular activities—soccer, tennis, piano, swimming, taekwondo—that they don't have time to sleep or read, let alone to think or daydream.

It's so easy to get caught up in our frenetic, overscheduled American pace that we inadvertently deprive our children of what they need most: our time and attention, the opportunity to be creative, to breathe and grow, to be grounded in the natural world and living systems, to have a connection with extended families and other cultures, to love and be loved.

Combating the "Toxic Commercial Culture"

How did this happen, and what can you do about it?

Corporations—which aggressively market to children products ranging from toys to junk food to tobacco to alcohol to violent entertainment—have created what Gary Ruskin, director of the Oregon-based Commercial Alert, calls "a toxic commercial culture that is purposefully damaging to children." In Ruskin's report to the World Health Organization Conference on Health Marketing and Youth in 2002, he says, "It is perhaps the first time in human history that adults have turned on their children and created a culture which harms not nurtures them." This "corporate-made culture," Ruskin says, "has shoved aside local cultures, local values and old ways of teaching health to youth."

Since consumerism is our dominant culture, anyone who consciously makes simple-living parenting choices in America today is in a sense countercultural—going against the tide. By making independent choices for your family, you are taking on battles that you might not have to fight if you fell into line with the culture of consumerism that puts out the message that more is better, that newer is best, and that, when in doubt, buying something will fix the problem. Marie Sherlock, author of *Living Simply with Children*, puts it succinctly: "If you're raising children in North America today and you're not consciously addressing the effects of commercialism on their psyches and beliefs, then you've essentially handed your child's soul over to corporate America."

In this chapter, we'll lay out nothing's-too-small choices that will help create a fire wall between your children's souls and the reaching fingers of corporate America. We'll suggest ways to nourish your children and empower them to achieve their full potential. Helping children discover their true selves—rather than grafting on some prepackaged four-color identity—should be among every parent's highest goals. We believe that by thinking for yourself and, by extension, educating your children about values, guiding them to manage their money, scheduling them appropriately, and planning and hosting celebrations in the right spirit, you will be setting the stage for well-groundedness and a lifetime of genuine success.

Not long ago—last November, to be exact, three months into his year as a first-grader, on the run-up to Christmas—Henry came up with an idea. A wonderful, awful idea. Henry decided that he wanted to "teach" me.

"Sit down, Mommy. Pay attention," he said. And pretty soon, his imagination caught fire, and the "classroom" at home grew to be occupied by not only me but by a whole slew of adults.

"Lesson one," he said. "This is a class about believing. Do you believe in Santa Claus? Do you believe in ghosts? In goblins? Do you believe that the wind has a voice of its own?" Empowered by his fantasy of being boss of the classroom, he was firing questions my way, not leaving me much room to respond.

Soon, he came to the heart of his lesson: "It's better to believe than not believe. Even if you can't see something or feel it, that doesn't mean it doesn't exist."

Doubtless, Henry was struggling with the concept of Santa Claus, fighting to hold onto his belief despite what the naysaying nine-year-olds he had encountered on the playground and at church had put forward. Wasn't this the most creative, original, talented six-year-old who ever walked the face of the planet? Naturally, as his mama, I thought so. For all the moments we parents have in which we fret about our children's missteps, about their boisterous interruptions in class, their bossiness with teachers and peers, their troublemaking tendencies in the lunchroom, moments like this—when they are *creating*, pure and simple—are nirvana.

Simple Living Family Values

In researching her book *Living Simply with Children*, Marie Sherlock compiled a list of values that self-identified simple-living families espouse:

* Compassion
* Love
* Family
* Community
* Respect for people and the earth
* Social justice
* Harmony
* Honesty
* Generosity
* Understanding
* Cooperation
* Peace
* Nonmaterialism
* Kindness
* Tolerance
* Diversity
* Responsibility

On top of my sheer glee with his form of play, I was taken with his idea of setting up a class to teach *adults*. I could see it now, all over America—six-year-olds assembling groups of paunchy, jaded, humorless adults, people who have had some of the life knocked out of them. The fact is, adults *can* learn much from children about what it means to be human. Wouldn't we all benefit if we could learn to live in the present, to delight in simple pleasures? If only we'd all pay attention, we might regain a measure of our humanity. Much of what children would teach us involves simplicity. Simple lessons about basic questions like this one: Do you believe? Looking at life through a child's lens could help adults reframe our thinking and put some idealism and light back into our lives.

But though we *can* learn from our children, the fact remains that we cannot shift all responsibility to the next generation. They are not grown, even if they appear incredibly mature at ever-younger ages. As I've heard Frank say more than once to Henry, "You may be smart, but you're not yet wise." It is our job as parents to lead the way. And with the pressures of a national time famine, and of the creeping and pervasive commercialism that has even penetrated the once-sacred territory of America's schools, how can we accomplish this?

Getting Started

As Marie Sherlock writes, when you make a decision to simplify your life, it's not a black-or-white thing. You position yourself somewhere on a continuum. Back-to-the-landers would be at one end and those who're living largely "traditional" American lives circa 2004 but who want to add some simple-living accents would be at the other. So don't think you'll immediately need to renounce life as you know it by making the decision to simplify.

Do try out some of the ideas in this chapter. If one doesn't work for you, look at some others. A good way to get started is to initiate a dialogue on values and simplicity with your family and children.

1. Talk about values

Take a Saturday morning over pancakes or an afternoon at the beach or out in the country and set aside some time with your family to discuss what's important to you. Conduct your meeting formally, like a business or club gathering. Limit your first discussion to no more than an hour. During this, use a flip chart or a dry-erase board. What kind of family are you? What do you believe in? If you're so inclined, draft a family mission statement. As a family, do you have goals to which you can point?

2. What do you like and admire in others?

What religious, political, military, or historical figures do you most admire, and why? In my childhood home, I grew up on the gospel of Margaret Fuller, the nineteenth-century feminist and women's rights advocate, as she was presented by my university professor mother, who made the study of Fuller her life work. The muse of Margaret Fuller—with her pioneering scholarship and political activism—encouraged us girls to pursue singular careers.

Today, Frank and I follow politics avidly. We admire people who work to make a difference—environmentalists, artists, activists, and others. We are also partial to friends from all phases of our lives—old college friends, people whom we've gotten to know at the annual Simplicity Forum Congresses around the nation, friends and colleagues in publishing, old buddies from our Hollywood days. And I must say we have a special fondness for members of our own local community.

3. What is your family known for, or what would you like it to be known for?

Robin Siegal of Los Angeles has three teenagers between the ages of twelve and eighteen. She says that her family is known for its philosophy of simplicity and practice of frugality; her affluent relatives were startled by the fact that her family spends no more than four hundred dollars a year on new clothing, most of it on shoes for the children.

Other families are known for their generosity, monetary or otherwise. The Levering family that I married into—specifically, Frank's parents—were known for being the kind of people who would give the shirts off their backs to those in need. They practiced those values for years, and their legacy continues to beam positive light on us after their deaths. For example, in 1950, Miriam and Sam Levering brought to the orchard a dispossessed, motherless Russian family with three children roughly the ages of their own. Then, instead of six children to care for, Miriam had nine.

If, for instance, your family admires volunteering but is not putting any time into it, you need to take a careful look at your life from a whole-systems perspective with an eye toward change.

4. Words into practice

Once you've determined your family values, you'll need to work with your children on how to put your philosophy into practice. Of course, how you accomplish this will vary tremendously when you're dealing with four-year-olds versus fourteen-year-olds. If one of your family values is frugality, for instance, and you buy used clothing for your child whenever possible, you're not likely to encounter a peep of protest from your four-year-old. But the fourteen-year-old may be a different story, especially if simple living is a new concept for her. If she's used to big hauls at the mall, you may need to simply talk to her and discuss the rationale for buying used clothing. She's growing and won't need this item long; it's cheaper and will save the family money; it's more environmentally friendly, since there's no excess packaging to throw away. Perhaps she can think of other reasons, and other uses for the money that's being saved.

5. *Needs versus wants*

This is a fundamental category when it comes to educating young people about simplicity. Given the overweening influence of television on our culture, an important distinction to impress upon your child is the difference between needs and wants. She *needs* food, shelter, clothing, and love to grow up strong and healthy, but she may *want* the latest Barbie doll, the trendy boots, and twenty-dollar bills for outings with friends. If she does not get these wants, there will be no dire consequences, especially if her self-esteem is strong. But sometimes fulfilling the wants can stress a family budget, putting it in jeopardy of not properly providing for the needs. And even if your family assets are as substantial and solid as Fort Knox, providing your child with her every want sets up an unhealthy early relationship toward money and things. It might cripple her future work ethic by establishing a sense of entitlement and the idea that she doesn't have to work for what she gets.

At six, Henry is not too young to experience this wants-versus-needs conflict. Early on in his first-grade year, I realized that though we could afford to buy him school lunch at $1.65 per day, it would be better for a whole host of reasons to pack his lunch. We'd save money, the food quality would be generally superior (or at least I'd have more control over it, packing more fruits, vegetables, and whole grains), and we'd reduce his personal waste stream. As a "packer," Henry would transport his lunchbox back and forth without having to toss one of the cafeteria's standard-is-sue, single-use foam trays into the garbage every day. And he could bring home stray carrots and any other leftovers for later consumption.

I assumed he was just as delighted with this arrangement as I was until he recently requested that I pack him a "cool lunch" like a Lunchable—a product with eater-friendly nuggets of processed ham, cheese, or turkey, along with cookies and the like, housed in a plastic throwaway tray. I have all kinds of concerns about this type of product: I question the additives in the food; I question the price tag for the amount of food you're getting; and I question the one-time use of plastic. So I explained to Henry that what he wanted was expensive and that we would hate throwing all that plastic away. I told him that when I pack his lunch, I pack a little love to go along with it. And I do. In addition to the meal I put together for him, usually in a plastic bag (which he dutifully brings home for reuse), I'll put in some small, sweet treat like a cookie, yogurt-covered raisins, or a handful of grapes, along with a little paper cutout heart that says, "I love you, Henry—Mom."

Simplicity at School

Simple-living values are a lot easier to sell your children on when you're the total—or at least the majority—influence on their lives. Unless you plan to home-school your children, once they get to school, they quickly begin to assimilate the values of their peers and their teachers. In this new world, the cultural norm *is* the norm. In many places, used clothing and homemade gifts and meals can start to look might shabby in comparison to what the other kids have. In fact, once your children are enrolled in school, you'll have a lot of new challenges to face as a simple-living parent—everything from peer pressure to too much homework to creeping commercialism.

Peer Pressure

Henry's lunch-packing issue is the tip of the iceberg with regard to the material (and nonmaterial) pressures children face as they make their way through school. It starts with small stuff like lunches and clothes and pretty quickly progresses to your vehicle, the size of your house, and your control over their schedules, activities, and friends. Henry knows that in Mount Airy, a shiny new SUV is the "cool" vehicle of choice. Setting aside environmental considerations, it's easy to understand his reaction. These behemoths lift passengers high off the ground. They appear big, powerful, and invincible, like a grand chariot in a race.

I am not an absolutist and would not want my child to be ostracized for following my lead. But on the other hand, being different from his peers will build your child's character and help him form opinions that may be at odds with those of the crowd. This is the kind of character that will come in handy later in life when weightier issues are at stake. If, as a child, you were the only one in the class whose parents drove a battered vehicle (that would describe Frank and me as children), and you survived, you might be better equipped to stand up against injustice later in life. You also might be less likely to panic if your financial fortunes take a nosedive, and you might have a higher tolerance for risk—professional or otherwise—than many others. You might be more inclined to think for yourself, and you might be less fear-based.

More Land and Your Land

The following story was written by Carol Holst as a parable to help young children begin to understand the concepts of "enough" and "too much." Before she became the director of Seeds of Simplicity in Los Angeles, Holst was a childhood educator. When read out loud, this story will spark much interest and discussion with your children. It is meant for preschoolers, kindergartners, and first-, second-, and third-graders.

On a day like today, in a place not far away, there was a land called More Land. It was called More Land because many of the grownups and children always wanted to have *more* of everything they could get. They wanted more food than they needed to eat, more clothes than they needed to wear, more toys than they needed to play with, and more houses than they needed to live in. The people in More Land even had special machines called Grabbers that brought them more of whatever they wanted whenever they wanted.

But the children knew that there was something wrong in More Land. No matter how much the people had, they were not happy—they always wanted even *more*! They did not care as much about each other and their land as they did about their things. And they were always thinking about money because they thought they never had enough.

Now, the children in More Land had a special mouse friend, and as it happens, her name was Enuf. Enuf was smart. She told the children about another land far away called Your Land. In Your Land, people were happy most of the time because they cared a lot about each other and took care of their land. They saved their money because they knew that they had enough things already. They knew that simple living was more important than having Grabbers. Enuf said, "You kids can show the grownups what to do! You can help turn More Land into Your Land."

So the children decided to surprise the grownups and tell them that they didn't need so many toys after all. The grownups were amazed and decided that they didn't need so many things either. The people in More Land started to feel much happier because now they had more time to enjoy family, friends, and nature. They didn't even use their Grabbers anymore. Peace and love filled the land, and soon More Land also was called Your Land.

Since the Grabbers were just standing around now, the children decided to give them to Enuf. "Thank you for helping us," they said. "Maybe you can think of something to do with these old Grabbers."

Well, the story doesn't have to end here. What do *you* think Enuf decided to do?

And don't forget that your child's independent thinking will impact others in his or her class.

Commercialism at School

"Many teachers and parents intuitively realize that excessive consumerism is not beneficial to children's emotional, mental, and physical health," writes Carol Holst in *Young Children: The Journal of the National Association for the Education of Young Children.*

Having a child in the public schools, I immediately noticed creeping commercialism in the educational arena. And it's not just the brand names that kids wear or want to wear, it's the way in which corporate interests get their feet in the doors of cash-strapped school systems. Unless their radar is extremely well tuned to the dangers of creeping commercialism, even well-meaning teachers and administrators can buy into it.

A case in point is the "Boxtops for Education" program by General Mills, which is in our local schools. Henry is encouraged to bring from home box tops to earn points for his classroom and ultimately more products (such as computers) for the school. This box-top campaign is billed as a fund-raiser. And of the eight first-grade classes at Tharrington Elementary, Henry's class is currently in the lead position. As a result, every time we go to the supermarket, Henry, in trying to please his teacher, nags me to purchase these products.

Talk about putting a parent into a position of conflict. On the one hand, I want Henry to respect his teachers and authority figures and to be able to work well within the system. On the other hand, I wouldn't ordinarily purchase most of these products. Many of them strike me as being overprocessed, overpackaged, and overpriced. If cereal's on my list, instead of Cheerios, I'd rather buy generic.

But I have caved a few times. And the last laugh was on me. When Henry wouldn't even eat several products he coerced me to buy—guess who was stuck eating the stuff?—I told him that we would support some programs in the school, but not all of them. The box-tops program had become box-bottom for me. Perhaps to compensate, we threw ourselves with zeal into the canned-foods giveaway program at Thanksgiving.

If you are concerned about such in-school campaigns, try speaking to teachers, principals, and the PTA about coming up with alternate fund-raisers. I've even heard some parents comment that they'd rather just make an outright donation to the school at the beginning of the year and not be pestered with all these fund-raisers. And even if Boxtops for Education or programs like it are not offered in your child's school, it's a good idea to speak to people in charge about preventing the problem of "commercial creep." Even better, get a group of parents to put it on the agenda at a PTA meeting and see if you can make your child's school or district a commercial-free zone.

Education Outside the Classroom

Just by living with you and being young and impressionable, your child is absorbing an education by osmosis. There are many things you can do to enhance your child's away-from-school education.

First, you can use TV as an educational experience. Most of us are aware of the dangers of television—both the sheer quantity of viewing and the exposure to commercial messages (see the "Thoughtful TV Consumption" section below). But you can use television positively. Select programs carefully, watch them with your child, and discuss them later. Henry and I have favorite videos, such as *The Sound of Music*. And sometimes when we need a pick-me-up, we'll put it on. Once, when we decided we wanted to learn the words to "My Favorite Things," Henry and I stopped and started the video until we'd jotted down all the lyrics and committed them to memory.

It's also important to try family volunteer service. Getting involved in community service will offer your child the best sort of positive modeling. (For more on this subject, see chapter 6.) If your volunteer work focuses on basic needs such as hunger, housing, and the like, this will help your child understand that others may be less fortunate but no less worthy. Your child may start dreaming up ways to help.

Frank and I are pleased that Henry periodically offers up toys to Goodwill and always makes a point to put in a coin at the Salvation Army kettle during the holiday bell-ringing season. Doing good for others also brings you closer as a family. If you give your child the idea that volunteering should be a part of his life, and then do it yourself, chances are good that you'll raise a lifelong volunteer. From volunteering, your child will learn some other important fundamentals.

1. Interactions don't have to be monetary

One of our pet peeves with American life today is the increasing monetization. People ask for dollars at every juncture, instead of joining into the spirit of human interaction and reciprocity. When your child sees you volunteer and sees that you like to do things for the sake of doing them, and not for dollars, he will tend not to monetize every act. He won't try to shake you down when you ask him to take the garbage out, nor will he expect payment when you ask him to help move Granny's couch.

2. Put life in perspective

Your child will learn to be less self-centered when she volunteers. Volunteering will inoculate her against a myopic, "I'm first" sense of the world. She will learn that the world is bigger than Oak Street and that she is not the only one with needs. When children are exposed to problems that should be shouldered by the entire community, they gain a healthy perspective.

3. Create happiness

As Habitat for Humanity International founder Millard Fuller told us recently in Mount Airy, "The happiest people I know are those who volunteer, who take on someone else's load, who don't wake up in the morning saying, 'How am I going to amuse myself today?' " Involving your children in volunteer work is a way of providing tools for their future happiness.

4. Take responsibility

Increasingly in our culture today, people want to point a finger elsewhere to assign blame for problems. Volunteering is powerful because it counteracts the notion that "it's not my problem." Volunteering lets children know the power of one or two, while reinforcing the message that nothing's too small to make a difference. It is living proof that you shouldn't sit on your duff complaining. Don't waste your time. Take action. Do something.

5. Learn tolerance

Because my late father was a lifelong chain smoker, I have always had an aversion to cigarettes and a fear that Henry will develop the habit. I believe Daddy would have lived well into his nineties—he'd be alive today!—had he not smoked. (Sadly, he died in 1996, the year before Henry was born.)

I've always tried to impress upon Henry, from a tender age, the dangers of smoking. A surprising problem has arisen: Henry is still young enough to take me literally, and too young to readily distinguish between private warnings and public proclamations. More than once, I've had to stop him from pointing at smokers and telling them to their faces that smoking is bad and that they should quit.

Community work can help teach your child the lesson that others—in this case, smokers—may not share his values or behaviors, but that their lives are just as valuable, and that he needs to be tolerant of the differences. Their skin color may be different. They may live in different neighborhoods, eat different food, smoke, and do things he doesn't, but your child should love them anyway. They are human beings worthy of respect and love.

Environmental Education

We take Henry along with us when we cart cans, bottles, plastics, and paper to the recycling center, and he loves helping unload. And now he's learning to pick up aluminum cans whenever he sees them, which we save and sell for a dollar or two per giant bagful at Mount Airy Iron & Metal. Henry picks up litter and pops it into trash cans on the street.

Environmental education involves informing your child why it's important to turn out the lights (to save energy and money) and why it's important to drive fuel-efficient vehicles or to walk or take public transportation whenever you can (to save fuel and minimize pollution). Try the following ideas to underscore your commitment to environmental stewardship and instill its place in the next generation:

1. Walk to school

If you live within walking distance of your child's school but tend to drive her or put her on a school bus, set aside some time one morning and walk her to school. It will be a fun jaunt for you both and will enable your child to see more closely the places she generally breezes by. When she sits down at her desk that morning, her blood briskly circulating from the walk, she'll be alert and ready to learn.

One Woman's Cans

Student Emily Garr has made diverting recyclables from the landfill a one-woman crusade on and around the Emerson College campus in Boston. Emily believes that Emerson's decision to recycle only paper—not bottles and cans—is "unacceptable and unnecessary." So she and a few friends have taken action. Informally, they set up collection containers on their dorm halls, and she and friends take weekly trips down the street and place what they have collected in the residential bins on nearby Beacon Hill.

Emily carries trash bags with her whenever she's out walking and gathers up anything that can be recycled. "I look at it more as an awareness activity than an actual action," she told me recently at a gathering of young college activists in Cambridge, Massachusetts. Emily believes that we should know where what we consume goes. "Let's not just put it in the trash and forget about it."

---

2. Try an electricity-free night

A big family adventure is to try an electricity-free night. You can go camping in the backyard, or you can stay indoors, turn off the lights, eat cold sandwiches, and do nothing involving television, the computer, or CDs. If you can manage it, turn off the heat or air conditioning and adjust your clothing to make yourself comfortable. By candlelight, tell stories, sing, make your own music, or sit on the floor and do a giant jigsaw puzzle. What a great adventure! Your kids will love you for it.

Outdoor Education

You'll read in chapter 7 about the "earth gym," a free outdoor physical-fitness training arena. Similarly, the "earth classroom"—or the great outdoors—is available free of charge, no reservations required, to all parents and their children. Nature, after all, is both mentor and healer to us all. Kids love being outdoors, running and playing and discovering the endless wonders of nature. But too often, we spend so much time in the car shuttling them between activities, or so much time indoors feeding on canned media, that we all but ignore God's great outdoors. A lesson in outdoor education can run the gamut from a simple stroll or jog outdoors to a leaf-gathering jaunt to a bona fide nature walk in which you or someone else points out plants and wildlife. Henry can easily while away a happy hour or more in a mound of dirt digging up rocks.

Take on a seasonal project with your child, like planting and tending a garden. She'll love to help you plan it, select the seeds, and lay it out. Assign her specific duties, like weeding and watering the plants; this is good discipline for your child and will help her learn responsibility. One warning: Don't get overly ambitious. It's better to start small and be successful with a modest plot—or even a potted patio garden—than to plan a quarter-acre spread and give up when the garden gets away from you in mid-July.

The Pfeiffer Center: Overcoming Kids' Fear of Nature

You may be surprised how receptive your child is to learning outdoors. A friend of ours from Mount Airy, Mary Woltz, worked and lived for a time at The Pfeiffer Center for biodynamic education in Chestnut Ridge, New York. Among her duties was working with kindergartners and second-, fourth-, and seventh-graders in the East Rampapo Central School District, exposing them to nature at the farm. The year she worked there, well over four hundred children experienced composting, sowing, planting, cultivating, harvesting, animal care, and ecology walks at the farm for three days during the school year.

As a resident beekeeper, Mary introduced the children to the hives and helped them overcome what she found to be a disquieting resistance to the natural world. "I'd hand them a bee to hold, giving them a drone," she recalled. Even when the children were told that the drones, or male bees, were not able to sting, they were still fearful. Another test came when she held up a honeycomb to see which child would be willing to stick a finger in for a dab of honey. Generally, the children were standoffish until one courageous soul stepped forward. Then the others would follow suit.

Outdoor education often gives the children of new immigrants "a chance to shine in front of their peers," Mary said. Children born outside of the United States would often brag that their grandparents had bees and large gardens where nature was deeply integrated into their daily lives. "You can see how much more connected to the earth these children are."

Outdoor education programs like the one at The Pfeiffer Center are great successes because they connect children with the natural world—many of them for the first time. One thing that made a lasting impression on Mary was how much the children enjoyed farm chores. "They got to do work—imagine that!—make cider, weave mats, understand what it's like to harvest food," she said.

But you don't have to own a farm or even enroll your child in a formal farm program. Just try out some of these ideas with your kids in your own backyard. You may be delighted by how engaged they become, how much work they can accomplish, and how they might even *enjoy* chores.

"Edible Schoolyards"

A wonderful idea that can bring the outdoors right to your child's school is an "edible schoolyard." Edible schoolyards—where schools create and maintain organic gardens and edible landscaping—are already in place in schools throughout the country. Students are involved in planting, harvesting, preparing, and eating the foods they grow. This hands-on learning experience helps them learn the principles of ecology, basic gardening skills, and essential nutritional information. It also connects them to the outdoors and the community and creates an awareness about conservation and land-stewardship issues.

A testimonial about the power of an edible-schoolyard project in Berkeley, California, came from teacher Joy Osborne. "At first my primary interest was looking for ways to enhance my students' understanding of the Neolithic period," she told an interviewer for the handbook *The Edible Schoolyard*. "Over time, I began to see that there was much more going on—we were cultivating a sense of community through our kitchen work. . . . We were coming together as a kind of family." Other teachers observed that clipping hedges together and pulling weeds often drew out shy, introverted students, giving them a sense of purpose and common mission. Plus, at the end of the day, students had something tangible to show for their efforts: the tasty and healthful fruits of their labor.

For more information on starting such a project at your child's school, do a web search using the keywords *edible schoolyard*. Or write the Center for Ecoliteracy at 2522 San Pablo Avenue, Berkeley, CA 94702 or visit its website at www.ecoliteracy.org. You can also write Virginia Tech Horticulture Department, Office of Environmental Horticulture, 407 Saunders Halls, 0327, Blacksburg, VA 24061-0327 or visit vtmg@tv.edu.

Money Management and Buying

Drawing on empirical data, Knox College associate psychology professor Tim Kasser, in his book *The High Price of Materialism*, demonstrates that those who place the accumulation of wealth and possessions at the top of their life goals put themselves at risk for unhappiness and health risks such as depression, anxiety, and intimacy problems. As your child's first and most influential teacher in matters of money management, buying, and consumption, it is your job to help her establish priorities and patterns that she can employ throughout her lifetime. "When [materialistic values] guide our behavior," Kasser writes, "our children watch and soak it up. Evidence suggests that children's value systems develop in part through imitation of what their parents value."

Of course, your first job is to put your own financial house in order by paying off debt, getting your spending under control, saving money, and planning for your financial future. (For more on money and consumption, see chapter 2.) But let's assume that you've done this, or that, like most of us, you are on the path to financial literacy and sound money management. How do you fight the pull of mainstream consumption and help your child learn the value of saving, of conscious consumption patterns, of minimalism?

The following are some tips that may help teach your child responsible money management:

1. Remember, you are constantly teaching your child about money matters

Though sit-down sessions about money are valuable, never forget that you're teaching your child every day of your life. Whenever you make a purchase when your child is with you, she is observing and absorbing your buying style. She may see you comparison-shop, shop from a list, or use coupons to save money. She'll see if you count change. Your child will take note if you negotiate for a lower price at a yard sale or on big-ticket items. She will most definitely take note of whether you cave in to her requests to buy impulse items at the checkout counter, and whether you reflexively defer purchases.

"Put it on your birthday (or Christmas) list," I tell Henry when he appears with something he "has to have," taken from one of those pandering displays designed to catch kids' eyes at the supermarket. Your child will notice if your approach to money is devil-may-care or more cautious and conservative. Once you understand this, you'll see that it's important for you to establish your own philosophy toward money and to consciously strive to achieve your goals.

2. Use allowance as a money-management teaching tool

When Henry entered first grade, we decided to start giving him an allowance of two dollars per week. He gets to spend it as he sees fit, though we try to encourage sound use of his money. Like many children, Henry has a tendency to be an impulse buyer, an I-gotta-have-it-now kid. When we were in New Orleans visiting a museum, he saw a spyglass set that he had to have. The item in question cost six dollars, or three weeks' allowance, and he'd already spent his allowance that week. After much discussion, we forked over the six dollars, with the understanding that over the next three weeks, any other requests for advances would be refused. That impulse buy followed him for almost a month; he'd shot his wad and couldn't even afford a piece of bubblegum. This lesson, as much as any other, has taught Henry to think long and hard about what he really wants to do with his allowance.

3. Money from chores

To supplement his allowance and the money he sometimes receives in greeting cards from doting relatives, Henry has started to earn money from household chores. The good news is that he really wants to work. He gets a dime for each commode that he cleans, and boy, does he ever put the elbow grease into it. (Yes, I know, I'm taking advantage of him at that rate, but in all fairness, when I was his age, I used to harvest great bags of asparagus from an abandoned garden near our home in Macomb, Illinois, and my mother paid me only a nickel—really low, even by 1960s wages.) As he ages, we anticipate increasing his work load, his allowance, and our offerings of jobs for hire.

4. Set up savings accounts and at-home funds

Since our trip to New Orleans when Henry went bankrupt temporarily, he has established a new fund—his rainy-day fund. Previously, we'd set up a college fund. The college fund consists of money that we deposit in the bank, money that we won't break into until he needs it for college; this money will presumably grow over time. The rainy-day fund is more immediately accessible; it's currently housed in an old eyeglass case of mine, and its contents are rarely bulging. From it, Henry can withdraw money for impulse buys anytime he chooses.

I've noticed that Henry likes having these funds. It makes him feel grown up and in charge to be able to direct where these dollars go. Often, when change remains from a purchase, he'll hand it to me and say, "Put this in my rainy-day fund."

5. Encourage part-time work

As your children get older, encourage them to seek part-time work and summer jobs and to save a portion of their earnings.

6. Make them pay the difference

As youngsters grow up and start to develop particular tastes (as in the aforementioned story about the clothing preferences of the four-year-old versus the fourteen-year-old), a commonly employed strategy among simple-living parents is to provide them with the minimum items. For instance, if a child needs a new pair of sneakers, the parent will provide the funds for an inexpensive pair bought at a discount store. If the child wants a fancy brand name, she has to earn the difference or withdraw it from her personal savings. It's amazing how much higher the bar is for a *want* when *her* money is at stake.

7. Reduce—or eliminate—brand names

I often think about my friend Merle, a colleague at the *Los Angeles Herald-Examiner* back in the 1980s, when designer jeans were all the rage. Merle had a policy against wearing any garment containing a visible brand name. Her idea took me by surprise at the time, especially when it came to T-shirts. But obviously, something about her idea resonated with me, as it has stayed with me so long.

Merle had a point. With children especially—whom marketers freely admit to wanting to "own" and to "brand"—it's a good idea to minimize brand-name clothing. And even if it's only symbolic, reducing the presence of brand-name logos around your home will lower the corporate influence in your life. It is also a statement that any person—child or adult—is a unique individual with innate self-worth. If your child isn't wearing the imagery and associations of particular brand names, it may be easier for you and others to access their unique identities.

8. Be generous

Frugal people are often stereotyped as being tightwads, but it's not necessarily true. Some of the most frugal people I know are also the most generous. They have bigger things to spend on than themselves. In his book *Prodigal Sons & Material Girls: How Not to Be Your Child's ATM*, Nathan Dungan espouses the "sharing-saving-spending" approach to teaching kids about money. "Sharing comes first," he writes, "because it offers the most effective counter rhythm for all the messages on spending. . . . Emphasizing sharing . . . counters the relentless message that 'stuff' makes the person." One of the reasons to be frugal and save is not for your own long-term goals but to help others.

Consumption Counts

You'll want to apply the same principles to teaching your child to be a responsible consumer that you did when you told him how to manage his money; many of the principles are interlinked. Work with your child to help him see through media-induced desires for consumption. Casually work into conversations your ideas—in your own words—about how all the striving for status-oriented products can detract from the best and most meaningful things in life, like feelings of being liked and loved, and of belonging and accomplishment. Feel free to share stories in which you made purchasing mistakes.

Here's one story I haven't told Henry, though someday I will. Once, I succumbed to temptation and paid too much for a hat that I saw in New York City. Since the hat cost more than I could really afford, I became preoccupied with losing it. And—guess what?—I did exactly that. I left it at a restaurant in the city by accident, and when I returned the next day to look for it, it was gone. There's a moral to this story: Don't buy things you can't afford. I knew that even as it was happening. Maybe it was a lesson I needed to relearn.

Tell your child that getting wrapped up in things often comes at the expense of other people and relationships—or, in my case, even being able to enjoy a pleasant, anxiety-free dinner.

In general, the following principles apply:

1. Less is more

Try to help your child understand that he can give more love to his toys if he has fewer of them. Point out to him how he has a few favorite toys, not three hundred.

Henry can relate to this point. His favorite toy is a stuffed animal named Gertrude, a yellow cat bought for him at Ray's Starlight Restaurant in Mount Airy in 1999 by dear friends visiting from Los Angeles, Ellen and Mal Hoffs. Henry is very protective of this limp, older creature, treating "Gerty" like an ancient great-aunt. Recently, he suggested we give Gerty a transfusion of stuffing from some of her plumper, younger plush brethren. He felt that might perk her up a bit. After all, Gerty has to survive so that his own children in the year 2027 can play with her.

Here's the thing about treasured items. In order to really treasure things, you have to remember something about them. And once you have more possessions than you can count on both hands and feet, or more than you could record on paper if someone asked you to itemize your toys, or more than you'd ever miss, you know you have too many.

2. Whenever possible, swap toys or buy used toys

You can do this at consignment stores, Goodwill, or yard sales. And tell your children why you're doing this: to save money, packaging, and the energy and resources used to produce new items.

3. If you must buy new, opt for items made from recycled materials

Children like the idea of earth-friendly products. In fact, logo-oriented kids love being the first to spot the recycled-contents symbol on packaging.

4. Consider hand-me-downs and clothing swaps

Add to the time-honored tradition of hand-me-downs the idea of a

---

Thoughtful TV Consumption

In our busy lives, the temptation to turn television into a babysitter is pretty overwhelming, and I seriously doubt that even the best-intentioned parents who own televisions haven't succumbed on occasion. After all, watching television is something kids generally *want* to do, and it does quiet them down for a while.

But the fact is that most Americans are watching way too much television. For impressionable children and teens, this "plug-in drug," as Marie Winn dubbed television, is exactly the opposite of what the doctor ordered. And now, with the proliferation of cable channels and niche programming, there is far more for parents to be concerned about—everything from graphic sex to grotesque violence to quick-cutting imagery that is exciting to watch but disturbs and distorts viewers' sense of time and reality.

What's more, the act of watching TV itself is troublesome. Robert Kubey and Mihaly Csikszentmihalyi, coauthors of *Television and the Quality of Life: How Viewing Shapes Everyday Experience*, say that viewers are put in a daze that makes it hard to shut the TV off. When they do, the lingering effect is lassitude. Watching television tends to foster lethargy and passivity, along with the desire for instant gratification and the quick resolution of problems. Prolonged viewing tends to give us unrealistic expectations about ourselves and the world around us. The characters on the tube tend to be wealthier, better looking, and happier than most of us. And I'm convinced that the catchy language of sitcoms and cartoons may adversely influence children's language and manners. There is research that even brain development, especially among the very young, is affected by television viewing.

Most of us are not ready or willing to go cold turkey and eliminate TV altogether for our children. Some experts say that, in our media culture, doing so would be a disservice. "Kids today are going to live all their lives in a media culture," Elizabeth Thoman, president of the Los Angeles-based social clothing-swap gathering. Get a group of families with kids together to swap clothes that they've outgrown. Anything left over might be donated to the homeless family shelter or the Salvation Army thrift shop.

Avoid Overscheduling

Now that you've looked at some of the essentials of reducing the impact of commercialism on your children's life and of giving them sound guidance on handling their money and becoming good consumers, you need to consider one other basic component that will help to simplify your life as a parent and theirs as children: avoid overscheduling. As William J. Doherty, coauthor of *Putting Family First:*

Center for Media and Values, recently told me. She believes that it's very important that children (and adults) learn media literacy skills.

The following are some tips that may serve as guidelines for making you and your child thoughtful television consumers:

1. Children under two years old should not watch television.

2. Children older than two should watch no more than two hours per day, and perhaps less on school nights, according to the American Academy of Pediatrics.

3. Whenever possible, watch programs with your children so that you can discuss the content afterwards. Ask them age-appropriate questions: Who made this program? Why? How do you feel about this show? And discuss the commercials in a similar vein.

4. Make TV a choice, not a habit. Whenever possible, preselect programs. If you can, use a television guide to chart out your week's viewing. Try to avoid turning on the set and surfing for something—anything—to watch.

5. Hide your television in a cabinet or put a blanket or cover over it when it's not in use, in order to minimize its importance in your life.

6. Never allow children to have television sets in their bedrooms. If they're in a "public" family room, you'll at least have some knowledge about what they're watching.

7. Make use of the VCR or DVD player. You can develop a library of positive programs your children will want to watch. One advantage to doing this is that, except for promos at the beginnings of the programs, there are no commercials with which to contend.

Successful Strategies for Reclaiming Family Life in a Hurry-Up World, says, "Families can only be a seedbed for current and future citizens if they achieve a balance between internal bonds and external activities." This balance, he goes on to say, has become "gravely out of whack for many families."

A return to time-honored traditions like meals together, bedtime rituals (and regular bedtimes), periodic family outings and nights, and plain, old, simple "down time" should be a priority for you and yours. The only obstacle to achieving this and putting back together your family life is your ability to say no to all the options and after-school activities that spring up. With your child's input, pick one or two extracurriculars and decline the rest.

Feel Like Celebrating?

Just when you think you've finally reached the young folks in your life—they've actually *heard* you about simplicity!—along comes the holiday season. Or a birthday. Or a prom. Or that mother of all celebrations, a wedding. Just when you think you've banished that beast of consumption to the outer darkness, back it roars with a vengeance, devouring all of your hard-won values in its path of spending, shopping, and harried preparations, threatening to swallow you and your children in a single gulp.

What's a parent to do? "The Christmas machine," as Jo Robinson and Jean Coppock Staeheli dub the monster in their book *Unplugging the Christmas Machine*, is a latter-day Grendel, the mythic beast faced by Beowulf. Few Americans emerge unscathed from the holidays, that long, winding tunnel of consumption and social expectation stretching from Black Friday—our national shopping holiday after Thanksgiving—till New Year's. Weddings—we average 2.3 million a year in the United States—can, like the Big Bad Wolf, blow your financial house down, running up an average tab of twenty-two thousand dollars. In the mad tug of war of peer pressure, even lesser financial fry—birthdays, proms, bar and bat mitzvahs—can become budget- and values-busters, celebrations where you take your stand and lose!

In the wake of these disasters, you rub your beleaguered eyes and survey the damage: new mounds of stuff to deal with, your simple-living intentions compromised, a family perhaps not as tightly knit as before, pulled from its center by the centrifugal force of materialism.

Must you always endure the excess? What actions can you take to reclaim the holidays, both for yourself and your children? How can you infuse the spirit of all celebrations with true gifts of the heart?

It's Your—Y-O-U-R!—Holiday Season

For all its potential charm, the holiday season has a way of dredging up disquieting issues from the psychic murk. This is especially true for that inner voice in many American women that Frank has dubbed "Ms. Perfect." As the holidays roll around again, Ms. Perfect begins to assert herself inside most women I know.

Ms. Perfect is the woman who does the holidays perfectly. Starting with the perfect wreath on the door, we enter the perfectly scented house to observe the symmetrical Christmas tree trimmed with ribbons, ornaments, and neatly strung tinsel. Ms. Perfect herself is preparing the perfect holiday meal, wearing impeccable, Christmasy clothes, complete with themed jewelry. Every minute on her calendar is scheduled from now till Christmas.

Core Values

If you agree that the holidays should not belong to Ms. Perfect, to the advertisers, or even to Santa and his elves, then what is the holiday season really about? When it comes right down to it, when you take away all the trappings, most of us believe that the holiday season should be personally meaningful, a time of renewal, a time to reaffirm core values and express family rituals. Ultimately, it belongs to us and our families and our faith.

Create Your Own Rituals

If this is how you think of it, why not create your own rituals, your own way of doing things, building on positive experiences you've had in the past? One way to start is by reflecting on the high moments from previous holiday seasons. Call a family meeting and ask your children what activities have brought satisfaction and joy. In your memory, what things have cast a warm glow across your heart? These are experiences to build on, activities that deserve a high priority.

By the same token, what things have you done in the past with your kids that didn't cut the mustard? Try to recall those times when you expected great things yet were disappointed. It's time to let go of those activities, even if they're traditions that go back years. The holiday season is busy enough already without burdening it further with hollow experiences that no one enjoys.

Ask your kids for their assessments. Follow the trail of all these reflections to a more meaningful experience the next time around. Ultimately, holiday rituals come down to choosing the kind of celebration you want. Meaningful activities with your children, personal renewal, reduced stress, the reaffirmation of values, and, for many people, spiritual truths—these are key aspects that many of us want from holiday celebrations.

What about you? What kind of celebration do *you* want?

Don't Be Afraid to Talk

Any parent knows that the holiday season is a humongous deal for kids. Our Henry, whose belief in Santa Claus was temporarily shaken but is intact again, knows that a year is divided, mysteriously, into two parts: the rest of the year and Christmas. Like all parents, Frank and I want to spin some childhood magic for him, and we shudder at the thought of not delivering on his holiday expectations.

The challenge, then, is to talk with Henry, to explain to him—repeatedly, if necessary—why we choose to celebrate as we do.

Communication of this sort is difficult enough among adults. When you celebrate the holidays differently from friends and family members—less materially, less frenetically—you have to overcome resistance to change. You have to *talk*. Sometimes, feelings get bruised. For example, a family member may feel defensive about the seven gifts she insists on giving Henry.

With a child—an utterly defenseless target for all purveyors of material things—conversation poses an even steeper challenge. Here are three "talking points" for your child during the holiday season:

1. Things (i.e., gifts) are not bad in themselves

The point is that too many of them—an excess—can give a child the false idea that more equals better, that excess equals love. The less-is-more concept is hard enough for adults, and it can be a really tough sell with kids. But it can be done. Even though we sometimes struggle with Henry, intellectually he grasps the concept that the gift he does receive is special, that it stands out and has great value for him because it is one of only a few, carefully selected gifts.

2. Love is time, and time is love

Kids understand this idea intuitively. They crave parents' time more than anything the world has to offer, but the bombardments of material culture tend to bury the idea under "stuff." To tell your child that your greatest gift is your time is to risk a puckered face and a curled upper lip.

One strategy that works for us with Henry is putting the shoe on his foot. Tell your child that his greatest gift to you is the time he shares with you. Make a game of it, pointing to your watch or a clock to illustrate. "Henry, do you think you could now give me a fantastic Christmas gift— an hour of your time? I know your time is really valuable, Henry, but I am craving one hour with you playing a game. Can you give me that gift, Henry? I know Christmas isn't quite here yet, but this could be an early Christmas present."

3. It's better to give than to receive

With kids, it's never too early to make a mantra of this age-old message and to model it in your own behavior. Take your kids to places where they will make a difference, like the proverbial soup kitchen or its many equivalents. Volunteering is especially important during the holidays. Community needs are greatest then, and so are your children's needs for perspective and giving back.

You Are Your Own Time Machine

To expand a bit on the subject of time, here's a fair question: Given all the demands of the holidays—decorations, food preparation, faith-based activities, parties, friends, etc.—how *do* you find time for your kids?

One of Henry's favorite movies is the original version of *The Time Machine*, in which, you may recall, a London inventor travels far into the future, where he meets the dreaded Morelocks. It's a fun film, but the question it raises for Henry's parents is this: How can we build a time machine that, rather than traveling into the future, creates more time with Henry?

This is a "timely" question always. During the holiday season, it's even timelier. (Okay, okay, I'll stop!) In addition to discarding activities that no one enjoys, consider setting a conscious limit on the number of outside commitments each family member can have. The net effect? Each family member will be pulled back to the center—the family's time together.

Giving gifts of time is another great way to build your family-time machine. Since Henry's an extroverted, never-met-a-stranger kid, one of the gifts he likes to give us is to perform improvised skits and "playlets," which often include made-up characters and songs. Since he is at once producer and director, these performances expand at his command to include all three of us!

Time gifts can be communal experiences—such as watching *It's a Wonderful Life* together, an annual ritual for us—or one-to-one experiences. To broaden the definition further, they may include taking the time to bake cookies, paint Christmas cards from scratch, or make homemade gifts—activities that are time intensive and that produce tangible results.

Here's another fun idea for time gifts: Formalize the arrangement in advance with a voucher that describes the gift to be given, the giver, the recipient, and, if appropriate, the date and time when it will be given. Kids love the ceremonial aspect here, as well as the anticipation of the event. To make the gift even more official, wrap it in wrapping paper—recycled, of course.

Uh-Oh, I Forgot the Budget!

The holiday season can be a budget-buster *extraordinaire*. According to Michelle Singletary, financial columnist for the *Washington Post*, "the average gift list consists of 10.5 people, and shoppers allot about $50 for each recipient." Other surveys point to even higher average expenditures. And when you have children, look out! The temptation exists to give them a plethora of material gifts, many of them impulse buys as you browse store shelves. "Dorian sure would like this," you say to yourself. "Britney would be thrilled to get one of those."

Budgets exist for a good reason: They keep our financial feet on the ground (see chapter 2). There's no better time than the holidays to teach your children the importance of a budget. According to InCharge Institute of America, a non-profit personal-finance and credit-counseling group, we overspend on holiday gifts more than in any other spending category. And because of our holiday binges, many of us spend months, even years, paying off holiday debts.

In general, the holiday season is a great opportunity to illustrate the fundamental time-money equation to young people. How many parents work extra hours during the holidays simply to buy their children more stuff? Those hours are time that could instead be spent with the kids—your best gift of all. And be sure to let your children know why you're choosing not to work those extra hours.

Birthday Basics

To paraphrase the classic song from the film *Casablanca*, the fundamental things apply—to your child's birthday. However, the focus really is on your child that one day in the year when she celebrates with loved ones the gift of life. For that reason, many parents and other family members are enticed into showering the honoree with extravagant material gifts.

Though material gifts in moderation have their place, as during the holidays, parents can choose other gifts as well. What's often harder for parents is convincing others to follow their lead. In our experience, it's extended family members and friends particularly who want to indulge Henry materially. In some cases, it seems it's partly to prove to us that they have their own, independent relationships with our son and can make their own decisions about what to give him.

The results can be unwelcome. Friction about values and who's in charge can contribute to a child's confusion about whose ideals and authority are in place. Conflicts of this sort can be difficult to resolve. But here are three ideas that in varying degrees have worked for us:

1. *Talk with the friend or family member* who doesn't share your philosophy about your child's birthday. Explain as carefully and as diplomatically as you can why you want to exercise some material restraint. Listen to the other side and express gratitude for that generous spirit.

2. *Encourage an experiential gift.* Why not suggest an afternoon of the person's time? Or a ticket to a play, concert, or sporting event? Such gifts don't increase the mound of possessions in your home (and your child's room), and they convey the message that learning and experiences are valuable in themselves. Creative family activities that generate great memories for everyone can be the best way to celebrate your child's birthday. Recently, Frank, Henry, and I spent several hours at a birthday celebration for another child at The Scrap Exchange in Durham, North Carolina. As did the honoree, Henry had a wonderful time making objects from various kinds of industrial scraps—wire, foam, bolts, etc.—that were donated to The Scrap Exchange by regional industries and made available for reuse in children's birthday parties and the like. Henry wants to return to The Scrap Exchange—maybe for his next birthday—and make another spaceship!

3. *Encourage the gift-giver to contribute to a fund* like Henry's college fund. Henry is proud of this fund and has learned to value it as much as material or experiential gifts.

I Thee Wed (Simply)

For years now, I've been hearing Frank's nostalgic "Quaker wedding" stories dating to 1962, when two of his four sisters were married only four months apart. Talk about simple weddings! One of Frank's sisters got married in the backyard of the "orchard house," as we call the home built by Frank's parents in 1939. Food for the meal afterwards was "furnished"—as the local expression goes—by the wedding guests, meaning that the wedding was potluck. Why not? Everyone in the Orchard Gap community was invited, as well as family and friends from around the country. The attire, Frank recalls, bordered on casual. Setting the standard for informality was the Blue Ridge neighbor who arrived in hair curlers. As Frank tells the story, when asked about the curlers, the neighbor replied, "I've got something really important to go to later today."

What's important, let's face it, is in the eye of the beholder! But most people would agree that a wedding is a pretty big deal. For you as a parent, your child's wedding can be the most important rite of passage in your relationship. Your son or daughter makes the last snip of the umbilical cord, and off he or she goes, destination unknown. Still, your influence will be felt long afterwards, and the wedding gives you a great chance to exert that influence—subtly, let's hope—through your values.

If you're a parent of the bride or groom, let your child know early in the planning stages that simple works for you. Even if you have the means for a blowout celebration, you might rather give your daughter and her future spouse a significant gift, rather than letting them blow it on one day. If, for instance, you'd be willing to contribute fifteen thousand dollars to your child's wedding, challenge her to put it on for five thousand and pocket the remaining ten thousand for a down payment on a house or car or to subsidize her education.

If you're the bride or the groom, rest assured that this is your wedding and that you make the final decisions. Fully 30 percent of American weddings are paid for by the couple getting married. If you prefer not to start your marriage trying to dig out of serious debt, you have every right to plan your wedding accordingly.

There are three keys to a simpler wedding: setting clear priorities, doing it yourself, and being creative and flexible at every step of the process.

1. Set clear priorities

When you think about your wedding, what are your top priorities? The ceremony itself? The wedding dress? Music for the reception?

Vital to a simple wedding is knowing what your priorities are. Start by making a list—in descending order, from highest to lowest. Forget about conventional thinking! What do *you* most want to accomplish? What are the things that matter the least to you?

This is the single most important thing you'll do. Knowing your priorities will determine where your energy and money will go. It will set you on the right course and set the tone for the entire experience, not only for yourself but for others as well.

2. Do it yourself

Sure, it's easier in many ways to turn the responsibilities over to "wedding professionals"—and those in the big-bucks wedding industry will be happy to oblige. But despite the hard work, attending to all the details of your wedding can be great fun. And what are friends for, if not giving you a hand as you prepare to take one of life's biggest steps? Bring them into the process early, and ask for plenty of volunteer work!

Once you've made your priority list, determine your overall budget. Figure out what you and anyone else participating financially will be willing to contribute. Then gather the friends and family who matter most to you and have a brainstorming session. Let them know what your total budget is, and work from there; otherwise, you'll likely spend a fortune. As Michelle Singletary said recently when she appeared with me on the television talk show *Moneywise with Kelvin Boston* on the topic "Having a Wedding without Going Broke," couples are often still paying off their weddings when they get divorced. Use that budget to inspire everyone who's helping you to think creatively. In every budget category, what can be done to both reduce the cost and provide something memorable, something distinctive?

3. Be creative and flexible

When I look back at my own wedding, what I remember most is the reception on the deck of the *State-o-Maine*, a Marine Maritime Academy ship anchored at Castine, Maine. As a wedding gift, my mother negotiated the rental of that deck for fifty dollars. Thanks to the view of Castine Harbor beyond the deck's railings, the live fiddle music, and the sea breeze gusting across the dance floor, it was a wedding reception that Frank, the guests, and I will never forget.

Weddings are your chance not only to be imaginative but to invite others to make that leap with you. What you are celebrating, after all, is a life force that is wildly imaginative beyond our ability to comprehend. A wedding celebrates the ability of two people to come together to overcome differences in background and, often, economic status. It's the imagination—not the lavish displays—that make a wedding distinctive.

As you plan your wedding, bear in mind that imaginative ways to do things can also be simple ways. As ideas come forward from friends, family, and your own imagination, stay flexible. A wedding, above all, should be fun. Beyond all the stress and friction that conflicting values and viewpoints may create, never lose sight of the fact that it's your wedding, your time to shine, your fun to be had, no matter what!

CHAPTER 6
Building Community

"Remember, no man is a failure who has friends."
—Clarence, the angel, to George Bailey,
the character played by Jimmy Stewart,
in *It's a Wonderful Life*

In the mad rush of America today, many customs that contribute to the quality of life have fallen by the wayside: homemade meals and the time to enjoy them; long, leisurely visits with neighbors and friends; taking time not only to smell the roses but to observe the seasons. However, one of the greatest casualties of modern times is the erosion of community life, something that was once at the center of our collective experience.

Indeed, in recent years, the loss of community connections and cohesion has jumped to the top of our national civic agenda, in part due to the high-profile work of Harvard professor Robert D. Putnam and his colleague Lewis M. Feldstein. Our national leaders have begun to recognize that the loss of community is not some distant and nebulous intangible, but a factor that concretely affects the quality of our lives. Recently, the term to express the value it represents—*social capital*—has entered into our national parlance.

Dr. Putnam's landmark 2000 book, *Bowling Alone: The Collapse and Revival of American Community*, makes the case that we Americans have become a nation of loners, and that this trend, if left unchecked, could shake the foundations of our democracy. Putnam cites declining membership in groups like the PTA, Kiwanis, and the Loyal Order of Moose, in churches, in book clubs, in garden clubs, in partisan political groups, and, yes, even in bowling leagues to demonstrate that we are increasingly pursuing "privatized" forms of leisure like watching TV and surfing the Internet, rather than connecting to others.

Technology Can Drive Us Apart

Technology—which enables us to do things individually that previously would have been done with others or in a public setting—is a major force separating us from each other. Today, we can listen on headsets to the musical selections of our choice without having to consider anyone else's taste. If we're away from home and need to make a phone call, we turn to our cell phones, rather than locating a pay phone. We surf the Internet for information and take classes online, never setting foot in a library or a classroom. We can bank online and withdraw cash from an ATM without making contact with another human being.

Though our lives have become increasingly peopleless, our hard-wired need for connections and emotions remains. Only recently have we begun to understand the high price we're paying for our isolation.

Rx: Community Involvement Boosts Your Health

The evidence is startling, compelling, and mounting: Community life is beneficial to your health, and not by a little but by a lot. Thanks to the people who study such things, we now have the medical stamp of approval for the fact that being involved in a group or organization is as beneficial to your health as quitting smoking, getting regular exercise, and eating better.

"There is a huge amount of public data that says incontrovertibly that connections make a huge difference," Lewis Feldstein, president of the New Hampshire Charitable Foundation and coauthor with Robert Putnam of *Better Together: Restoring the American Community*, told me when I recently met with him in Cambridge, Massachusetts. For instance, data shows that if you are not a member of a single social, civic, religious, or fraternal organization and you join one in a particular year, your chances of dying that year will drop by a staggering 50 percent. "If you join another organization that year, your chances of dying drop another 25 percent," he said. The effect levels off after joining two clubs. If you join too many, he cautions, you place yourself in danger of social overload.

"We know that, at some level, being connected is natural," he said. "It's a close call as to which would kill you first, smoking three packs of cigarettes a day or being all alone, literally."

The "Roseto Effect"

Public-health experts term the advantages springing from having strong community and interpersonal ties the "Roseto Effect," after a famous 1950s study of a group of poor Italian immigrants who moved to Roseto, Pennsylvania. These people, who were connected by strong community customs and ties, were noticeably healthier and longer-lived than their peers in nearby towns, with whom they shared risk factors such as poor eating habits, minimal or nonexistent exercise routines, and an addiction to cigarettes. As it turned out, their health edge wasn't genetic. As the next generation of Italian-Americans from Roseto assimilated into American culture and broke free of the tight-knit community ties of their parents and grandparents, their health advantages disappeared.

A plethora of research studies affirms the role of human connections and interactions in good health. One such study, conducted by a team of psychiatrists at Stanford University Medical School, led by Dr. David Spiegel, found that patients with metastatic breast cancer who joined support groups lived nearly twice as long as patients who received only medical care. Other studies have demonstrated depression to be less prevalent among women who maintain many close friendships.

"The fact that depression is now an international epidemic is reflective of these deep needs for connection that aren't being met," Frances Moore Lappé, author of *Diet for a Small Planet* and thirteen other books, told Frank and me during a recent visit to her sunny apartment in Cambridge, Massachusetts. These deep needs to feel connected, she explained, are fulfilled "through real sharing of experience and in common endeavor."

But why are the bonds that are formed from the sharing of experience and common endeavor increasingly hard to create and maintain? The answers are complex. Many Americans are either transients—people not closely connected to any particular community—or community dropouts whose lives have become increasingly self-contained. With more two-career couples in the workplace, and with many people working ever-longer hours and spending more time commuting, the lack of discretionary time is taking its toll on community life.

Some of these unconnected individuals may never have experienced the pleasures of community life and may even lack a vocabulary to express that void. Others feel an emptiness in their lives but can't put a finger on its source.

A decade ago, Ken Munsell of Ellensburg, Washington, told me he was convinced that the national resurgence of interest in small-town living was in part a result of the decline of community life: "People are missing something, and they don't know what it is." Now, ten years later, it's clear that what *it* is is community life.

Big and Little Things to Build Community

The first step to building community—and increasing our social capital—is recognizing its centrality to our overall health and well-being. "We need to start by getting people to say, 'Hey, this stuff counts,' " says Lew Feldstein. Once you decide that this stuff *does* count, you'll need to make a conscious effort to fold community building into your everyday life.

There are big and little things you can do to build community. Following are ideas that anyone can try; we're limited only by our time, energy, imagination, and initiative. Try one or two, or try them all. Remember, nothing's too small to make a difference.

1. Join a group

Given the preponderance of evidence about the health-enhancing benefits of joining a club, group, or organization, make it a point to join at least one group. Then take your membership seriously. Joining an organization with a mission—or even one with no more mission than providing fellowship—is a great way to get outside yourself. Clubs are meaningful meeting grounds for building community, networking, socializing, and establishing a goal or mission that can best be tackled by a group, rather than an individual. And remember, civic groups are the lifeblood of a community. When various organizations work well together, that's a good indicator that a particular community has a strong, well-lubricated civic infrastructure.

2. Learn people's names

Here in Mount Airy, employees at a successful local institution, the F. Rees clothing store, are all schooled in the art and importance of learning customers' names. Owner Gene Rees, who happens to be our office landlord, once told me that the key to learning someone's name is to make a mental note of it when you're introduced. During that first meeting, repeat the name as many times as you can, out loud and to yourself. Put the name itself on your conversational agenda. Ask how it's spelled. Spell it back to that person, and ask if he or she is related to someone else you know by the same name. Or tie it to a celebrity or a famous historical figure. The point is to go over the name, performing any mental gymnastics that will help etch it in your memory. Then, when you next see that person, say, "Hello, Holly. Are you having a good day?"

How Joining Rotary Changed My Life

It is not an exaggeration to say that joining the Mount Airy Rotary Club back in 1992 changed my life in a major way. It helped thrust me to the center of community life here in town. From the weekly programs, I've learned about the goings-on around our town and the region. And I've been able to socialize casually over lunch with people from different walks of life, many of whom I would not have had serious or regular contact with in any other context. Seeing people on a weekly basis and working with them on projects like quarterly roadside litter pickup has really helped to cement bonds. Serving on the club's publicity committee and helping to select high-school participants in the district's youth leadership camp program expanded my circle, my base of knowledge, and my community involvement. And joining Rotary opened the door into other significant volunteer groups, such as the Greater Mount Airy Chamber of Commerce, the United Fund of Greater Mount Airy, the All-America City Committee, and many others. It also gave me the chance to meet the cadre of committed community servants who call Mount Airy home.

Just as my former boss, Robert Merritt, invited me to join the club, bringing others in has been a pleasure. It was a thrilling moment for me back in 1994 when I inducted Monroe Watkins into the Mount Airy Rotary Club. His initiation represented two firsts for our club: He was the first representative of the day-care-center category, by virtue of owning several in the county, and he was the first African-American to join. I'll never forget the universal outpouring of affection and enthusiasm on the part of club members. And when my then-seventy-nine-year-old stepfather, Colonel Joseph B. Whittaker, moved to the area in 1996 after marrying my mother, he didn't know a soul. I am convinced that membership in Rotary helped this Pennsylvania native to enhance his quality of life before he passed away in 2003 at age eighty-five. Inviting Ann Vaughn, social capitalist *extraordinaire* and director of the Mount Airy Visitors Center, to join was also a highlight. I look for my Rotary friends every Tuesday over lunch. When one of my special Rotary friends is absent, I experience pangs of disappointment.

3. Make small talk

Successful merchants know that they can increase their sales if they engage would-be customers in conversation. Recently, when I had a few hours to kill during a layover at Washington Dulles International Airport, I was that customer. I strolled by a music stores called Altitunes and started browsing. James, the clerk on duty, asked where I was going. I was startled. In the frantic culture of major airports, I'd never once had a merchant ask me anything more probing than if I took my coffee black or with cream and sugar. We struck up a conversation, and I came home with a new CD. The moral of this story is not that friendliness boosts retail sales (though it can't hurt), but that we're so starved for connection that anyone who takes the time to ask questions and engage us in conversation will be rewarded, if not with a sale, then with a shared moment together—something we all crave.

And don't wait for others to talk to you. Extend yourself. When you go into the pharmacy or the home-improvement store, ask people you encounter a question or make a comment. Use your imagination. Ask the checkout clerk what her brand of toothpaste is, or ask her if she's still in school. Ask the assistant manager how long her shift is. Just think of something that will open the door to an exchange. And remember, when you talk to someone, really focus on that person. Don't be fumbling in your wallet or adjusting your bra strap. Train your eyes on the person you're addressing and give her your full, undivided attention. You may be making the most meaningful contact that person will have all day. I was once struck by the poignancy of an older woman who complained that, because of her lined face, people "don't even look at me anymore."

4. Listen more, talk less

Writer Brenda Ueland once observed that when we listen deeply to people, we experience "an alternating current" that "recharges us so that we never get tired of each other." In fact, the most community-oriented people I know do more listening than talking, and they are generally energized by what they hear. One of our leading citizens in town is endlessly curious about others, always asking questions, always taking in others' answers. He's a thoughtful listener who genuinely cares about what he hears. If you've ever talked to him, you'll know he's heard you because he'll drop something you've said into conversation months or years later. And don't forget that listening more than talking is a sign of emotional maturity. As the old saw goes, "Wise people know what they say; foolish people say all they know."

5. Be punctual

A great way to build community is to show up on time—or, better yet, *early*—to events, gatherings, appointment, lunch dates, and the like. This is a means of showing respect for the person who has invited you and for the event itself. Having a cushion of time will help put you into the right frame of mind for the experience and lay the grounds for your enjoying and being more completely present for it.

What Daddy Taught Me about the Art of Crossing Cultures

My late father, Edmund S. Urbanski, loved to mix it up with new immigrants to our country. And in doing so, he quite literally made their day. Now that I've studied the health benefits of social capital, I realize that such interactions made *his* day as well, which may be why he lived to the ripe old age of eighty-seven.

Before he retired, my father, a Polish expatriate who became a naturalized American citizen after he married my American-born mother in 1952, was a professor of Romance languages at Howard University in Washington, D.C. Because of his classical European education and innate skill, he spoke four languages fluently (Polish, English, Spanish, and German) and two languages well (French and Portuguese). For the record, he also studied and was proficient in Latin and Greek.

I have many fond memories of Daddy engaging in long and lively exchanges with busboys, taxi drivers, supermarket clerks, and sometimes total strangers near his home in Silver Spring, Maryland. Having once been an immigrant to this country himself—and having faced ethnic prejudice and the sad aftermath of World War II in his native land—perhaps he, more than most, recognized the profound importance of extending the hand of friendship to newcomers. My elderly, dapper, distinguished-looking father often startled Latinos when, out of the blue, over the produce counter at the supermarket, he would address them in their native tongue. More than once, he invited new acquaintances to his apartment or to a coffee shop for coffee, tea, and cake in the afternoon, as is the Polish custom.

At his funeral in 1996, there was a tremendous outpouring of affection for "the professor," as he was called, not only from friends and family in the Polish community in Washington but also from his Portuguese dentist, the Mexican maintenance man and the Haitian gardeners at his apartment complex, and many others whom his life had touched. They were sad to see the professor who had thought so much of them leave this life.

Though I'm no linguist, occasionally when I hear Polish spoken, I smile and greet folks with "*Dzień dobry*,"—"Hello"—which makes their day. And mine, too!

6. *Slow your pace*

Some great ways to slow your pace are by walking, biking, or even driving more slowly. When you do this, you will notice the little things that make up the collective landscape of your community: the new window display at the local florist featuring spring flowers or autumn leaves; an announcement for a blood drive posted on a bulletin board at the drugstore alongside a flyer for a potluck supper. A slower pace will also give you time to talk to passersby, both those you know and the ones you haven't yet met.

7. Help travelers and tourists

Mount Airy attracts its share of tourists, who come to actor Andy Griffith's hometown in search of the spirit of Mayberry. Most of them make a beeline for the Mount Airy Visitors Center on North Main Street, where they are greeted by executive director Ann L. Vaughn, social capitalist *extraordinaire*, or a member of her friendly staff. After they've toured the world's largest collection of Andy Griffith memorabilia, they wander up Main Street seeking out additional attractions—the Old City Jail, Snappy Lunch, the Bluebird Diner, and the Main Oak Emporium. Since our office is located on the second floor over a gift shop on Main Street, Frank and I often bump into map-toting tourists who sometimes appear a bit lost. On nearby City Hall Street, I often see husbands snapping shots of their wives (or vice versa) in front of the '62 Ford Galaxy, a duplicate of the patrol car on *The Andy Griffith Show*. Whenever I can, I offer to snap their pictures together. Talk about happiness! Nothing seems to delight tourists more. And I get a rush of pleasure by doing my part to offer old-fashioned Southern hospitality to strangers, with no expectation of reward. As a bonus, I always feel that I'm polishing the good feelings about our community that these tourists will take home.

8. Start a supper club

Breaking bread together is a surefire way to create community. Carolyn R. Shaffer, coauthor with Kristin Anundsen of *Creating Community Anywhere*, says that sharing meals "allows you to get involved in each other's lives and develop camaraderie." Ideally, a dinner club should meet every one to two weeks for a meal out or for a potluck at someone's home or a community center. This can be a group that shares a common interest—Presbyterian businesspeople, stay-at-home moms, creative writers, neighbors on Willow Street. Or it can be a diverse group of people of different generations, backgrounds, and income brackets. You'll be surprised at how tight-knit such a circle can grow over time, as people get to know each other. The optimal size for a dinner club is eight to twelve people. Be sure to schedule gatherings regularly—either weekly or biweekly, but no less than once a month. Otherwise, the glue holding the group together will start to lose its hold.

9. Host a dinner party

If you're not quite ready to make the leap to forming a supper club, why not host a dinner party? Just one. You may find you like entertaining so much that you'll do it more frequently.

In attempting to not only *study* social-capital formation but also to do his part to build community in and around Hancock, New Hampshire, Lew Feldstein transformed a television room in the home he shares with Mary McGowan into a giant dining room. He and McGowan started with one dinner party and now host one every month for twelve to fifteen guests. His is not a supper club, as the guest roster changes monthly. Though Feldstein and his friends may be partly responsible for the statistical spike in the number of dinner parties thrown in New Hampshire versus the rest of the nation—New Hampshirites give more dinner parties than do most Americans—the average number of dinner parties around

The Johnson Family Scholarship

Several years back, I met a lovely man named Melvin Johnson through the Piedmont Triad Leadership Network, a multicounty leadership training-and-development program in northwestern North Carolina. Dr. Johnson, who is provost and vice chancellor of academic affairs at the historically African-American Winston-Salem State University, related a creative concept that beautifully illustrates how you can build social capital within your own family. His brainchild? The Johnson Family Scholarship.

Here's how it works. Every year, the Johnsons meet for a reunion either near the family homeplace in Lincolnton, Georgia, along the eastern seaboard, or occasionally in vacation destinations like New Orleans or on cruise ships. Every year, along with the customary food, fellowship, and entertainment, the three-hundred-odd family members contribute a certain amount to the family scholarship fund. They supplement this kitty with profits from a self-published family cookbook. And just as a club or college evaluates scholarship applicants, the family appoints a committee of four to review applications. The only requirements are that the applicant be a family member and a high-school graduate who has been accepted into a community college, college, or university. The family has administered this program since 1993. During that time, more than thirty young Johnsons have received a total of approximately ten thousand dollars in scholarships.

With dollar awards ranging from three hundred to five hundred dollars, the scholarships clearly don't give recipients a full collegiate ride, but they do help with books and incidentals. "They're symbolic in importance," says Dr. Johnson. "Both the recipients and the contributors feel so much pride. You ought to see the grandparents and parents just beaming with pride in the students when we make the presentations."

Though the idea originated with Melvin Johnson, he modestly credits his and others' involvement in higher education as the real source of inspiration. "A lot of family members are involved in higher education," he says. "So this was a very good idea to stem out of our family values. One of those values is to foster scholarship and improvement in our lives. The way we look at it, there's nothing better than investing in our future, and our future is our children."

And the program has a fringe benefit: It invests scholarship winners in the family. "My own three children are all recipients," says Dr. Johnson. "We hope that this will encourage them as well as others in the family to give back as well."

the country has taken a nosedive in recent years. In the early 1970s, for instance, Americans invited others over for an evening meal seventeen or eighteen times a year, on average. That number has dropped over the three decades since to an average of *eight* times per year.

10. Consider co-housing

Living with others can be food for the soul and salvation for the pocketbook. The arrangement can be as informal as having a roommate or as structured as starting a group with common goals and values, a mission statement, and the desire to form a kind of "family" unit.

A student at the University of North Carolina at Chapel Hill purchased a home his freshman year and made the mortgage payment each month by renting out rooms throughout his college years. By the time he graduated, he had an equity nest egg with which to jump-start his adult life. This is a great strategy for an entrepreneurial freshman—or any enterprising person, for that matter—as long as you can come up with the down payment and have a stomach for screening renters, haggling over bills, unclogging toilets, and overseeing or doing repair work. What's more, strong environmental benefits accrue from group housing.

11. Turn off the TV and computer

If you can reduce the number of hours you spend in front of the television set and on the Internet, this will free up more time for community building.

As Janet Luhrs writes in *The Simple Living Guide*, "TV is educational, especially the ads: They teach kids to be self-centered, impulsive, and addictive." A recent national survey indicated that the average American watches 3.8 hours of television daily. If you watch that much or more, try to set your mark lower. Another strategy is to preselect at the beginning of each week what you intend to watch. Or consider going on a television diet for one week and seeing how that affects your quality of life. If one week's too much, put a blanket over the TV for one night a week, or leave the screen blank for 24 hours.

Likewise, people of all ages are spending greater and greater amounts of time surfing the web. What's often cut out is time for friends, family, the community, and even pets.

When you reduce your hours in front of these machines, you free up time to be creative and to live.

12. Read the newspaper

In what to me was a telling but disquieting moment of candor, an American president recently volunteered that he never bothered to read the newspaper, preferring instead to receive all his information directly from his advisers. His admission not only served to work against his wife's literacy campaign, but he inadvertently told the public that he was disconnected from the community as well.

Unlike television viewing, regular newspaper reading actually serves to *enhance* people's engagement in their local, national, and global communities.

13. Spend less time on the road

In studying declining social capital, Lewis Feldstein and his colleagues came up with what may appear to be a surprising finding: A direct relationship exists between the time we spend on the road in our vehicles and the time we devote to community life. It's called "the ten-ten rule." "For every additional ten minutes you spend driving in a car, it reduces by 10 percent virtually every form of civic activity," Feldstein told me in Cambridge. "You are 10 percent less likely to vote, 10 percent less likely to volunteer, 10 percent less likely to be trusting of your neighbors and of storekeepers, 10 percent less likely to eat meals with your kids." A surefire way to increase your community involvement is to reduce your commuting time. You could move closer to where you work or work from home part of the time. Using mass transit or carpooling will also give you more time to read the newspaper, write notes and letters, and visit with people.

14. Donate to worthy causes

Donate time, money, canned goods—whatever you can. Instead of begrudging solicitors for worthwhile causes, embrace them. Visualize yourself boosting good projects by your gifts. If you have problems staying within your budget, allocate a certain amount of money every year for donations, and then take pleasure in giving it. As one who has raised funds in the past for community groups and other projects, I know it's better to receive even small donations from many people than a multitude of "no's." And don't allow your inability to make a large gift stop you from giving. Even giving a check for five to fifteen dollars to a worthy cause will help advance it, to say nothing of boosting the morale of those collecting the funds.

I remember our friend, University of Maine wildlife professor and environmentalist Malcolm L. "Mac" Hunter, Jr., making the case that it's good to support as many worthy organizations as possible because it helps those groups to demonstrate a wide donor base. But perhaps the greatest reward for you is that when you give, you feel that you're part of something larger than yourself.

15. Attend town meetings

Go to town or city council meetings. Find out what the issues are and get involved. Once you learn about the questions of the day and the hour, you will find yourself following them more closely and feeling engaged in the political workings of your community.

Simplicity Circles

If you'd like to build community and simplify your life at the same time, consider starting or joining a simplicity circle. The simplicity circle movement started in the early 1990s in the Pacific Northwest and is now spreading throughout the nation. Akin to the consciousness-raising and women's groups of the 1960s and 1970s, simplicity circles are organized by people who want to simplify their lives and who meet regularly to cheer each other on, to address serious concerns, and to share practical information about ways of living better.

Cecile Andrews, author of *The Circle of Simplicity* and a friend of ours for many years, helped to launch simplicity circles back in 1992 when she taught a class in Seattle on the subject of voluntary simplicity. Her book, the bible of the simplicity circle movement, was published in 1997. In writing it and developing the simplicity circle model in this country, Cecile turned to the Scandinavians for wisdom. She based much of her work on Swedish simplicity circles and Danish folk schools. According to Cecile, the Danish folk-school movement was started in the 1860s by downtrodden peasants who decided to get together and educate themselves. A century later, those folk schools had helped make Denmark one of the most progressive countries in the world, with a high standard of living and literacy rate. Today's Denmark is a place that holds both people and the planet in high regard.

Cecile outlines the ground rules for starting a simplicity circle:

* Get a core group of two or three people to agree on founding one, then recruit six or so additional participants.

* Hold the meetings at one person's home, or rotate homes and locations. You can also hold your circle at a church, community center, school, community college, or library.

* A new circle should last for at least ten weeks. And it should meet weekly or every two weeks. After the ten weeks, the group may decide whether or not to continue to meet. Many well-established circles have been meeting for years.

* Information about how to proceed is available in *The Circle of Simplicity* and through Seeds of Simplicity, a national grass-roots organization based in Los Angeles. You can contact Seeds of Simplicity by calling 877-UNSTUFF or by visiting www.seedsofsimplicity.org.

* At each meeting, every circle member should commit to an action and agree to report back at the next gathering. It can be an action as small as donating an old winter coat or as large as looking for a new place to live. In any case, because individuals are accountable, they must report back to the group about what they have achieved (or failed to achieve). We all know how being accountable to others helps spur action.

You're the Expert

Back in 1997, I helped to start a simplicity circle in Winston-Salem, North Carolina, that met at the Reynolda House Museum of American Art. And though I've been working with Frank in the field of simplicity for decades—since the late 1980s, to be exact—what intrigued me about the experience was how fresh it seemed. It was exciting to meet a new group of people and to see them uncover their own insights about the need for simplicity in their lives and to learn how to implement change. It was especially exhilarating to watch a woman who had been caught up in the consumer rat race connect the dots and effect change in her life. I still remember her asking the group for advice on how to refuse her preteen children the fifty- and hundred-dollar bills they were used to blowing during an afternoon at the mall, as had been their custom before her divorce.

Carol Holst, who is the national director of Seeds of Simplicity and a dear friend of ours, says that the results "are based on people's own wisdom. That's the genius of the circles. Rather than having experts give us the answers, people empower each other to find the answers for themselves and share their wisdom and their stories."

The experience of a simplicity circle is what Holst calls "democracy in action." Circles are leaderless and egalitarian, she explains. "In this country, it's difficult to find an experience where there are no 'right answers,' and people are on an equal basis to discover for themselves and to share insights. People who are struggling to make decisions in their purchasing and in their use of the earth's resources can find sources of inspiration in what others are doing."

Volunteering

Because of the widening gap between the haves and the have-nots, and because of the increasing isolation in our society, we are experiencing a "desperate need for civic revival," according to John Saltmarsh, Ph.D., project director for Campus Compact, an organization that is working to introduce "service learning" to college campuses nationwide. The objective of Campus Compact, based at Brown University, is connecting students' community experiences outside the classroom with their academic study.

In the midst of our national civic crisis, many believe that the need for volunteer work to put our society back on track has never been greater. So what does it take to draw volunteers, and why should already overscheduled people add one more commitment to their lives?

If anyone knows the psyches of volunteers, it is our friends Linda and Millard Fuller, who back in 1976 founded Habitat for Humanity International in Americus, Georgia. Habitat has since grown into one of the largest service organizations in the world.

When I asked Linda Fuller during her recent visit to Greensboro College about the thread that links volunteers and the volunteer experience, she paused for a moment before answering. "You could sum it up with two words—building community." As houses go up, volunteers are not only erecting a structure, she said, but also "building friendships, building community, and building hope."

The fundamental building block of community is relationships. When you establish a relationship or make a friend, you step outside yourself and into the other person's shoes, consider his or her needs, and put that other person first. Volunteer service consists of formalizing the impulse to put another—or some higher cause—before yourself. Volunteer work goes to the heart of building community.

Linda Fuller said that with first-time volunteers—especially the ones who've led privileged or sheltered lives—it's fascinating to watch what happens when they meet the recipients of a future home. "You can almost see the wheels start turning," she said. "For some of these volunteers, they're surprised to see good, decent human beings—rather than their stereotype of a 'needy family'—on the receiving end of their volunteer work."

The Therapeutic Benefits of Volunteering

For years, volunteering has been thought to be the work of do-gooders and church people; all too often, it's been dismissed and trivialized as the work of little old ladies with too much time on their hands. But just as with being a community participant, it turns out that volunteering not only helps others but also delivers tangible benefits to the helper. For a whole host of reasons—from improving your health to expanding your circle of acquaintances—it's good for you to pitch in and put on your altruistic hat.

Numerous studies demonstrate the health benefits of volunteering, which include lowered blood pressure, increased self-esteem, lessened feelings of social isolation, a strengthened immune system, and reduced stress. Even a relatively small time commitment can make a difference, according to a 1999 University of Michigan study that identified the health benefits to senior citizens of less than one hour of volunteering per week. Volunteering is beneficial to everyone, but most especially to those who are out of the workplace, such as retirees, the unemployed, and stay-at-home parents or spouses. These people, who can easily become isolated, may reap the largest benefits because of the social connections that are forged in dishing out soup at a homeless shelter, tutoring a child with her reading or math, or organizing a rummage sale for charity. What's more, taking on an authority role may add esteem-boosting professionalism, mastery, and competence to one's sense of self.

Culture Extends Life

A research study from Umea, Sweden, demonstrated that participating in public cultural activities like concerts, films, theatrical performances, art openings, and, yes, even sporting events can add years to your life. A longitudinal lifestyle survey of more than twelve thousand people revealed that those who regularly attend such events are half as likely to die during a given period as those who do not. Why? Study supervisor Lars Olov Bygren believes that such events—where we rub elbows with others and participate in a collective experience—help to produce strong emotions among those in attendance, thus stimulating their immune systems.

The Michigan study found that, by providing a sense of purpose and meaning, volunteering contributes to a longer life. Volunteers of every age group benefit when they give back and engage in nonmonetary forms of exchange.

Other benefits include the following:

1. Having fun

Linda Fuller noted that, once exposed to the excitement of building a new house, Habitat volunteers often get so "high" that they want to keep on going. "Sometimes, it causes them to have to make a choice. 'Well, I've either got to go shopping with my friend or I'm going to work

High Social-Capital Communities

High social-capital communities are characterized by greater connectivity, trust, and reciprocity than other communities. In communities that achieve these benchmarks, data demonstrates that people are healthier, happier, and more prosperous, that the local schools and their students perform better, that citizens are physically safer and crime is lower, and that government is more responsive and works more effectively. In high social-capital communities, strong networks exist among people.

If you're curious about what life is like in two high social-capital communities, read on. And if you're inspired to bring some of these changes to your community, by all means go for it!

Tupelo, Mississippi, and Portland, Oregon, are two cities that consistently receive a lot of press for exhibiting strong social capital. Here's why:

The power of pulling together

Lee County, Mississippi (the county seat of which is Tupelo, the hometown of Elvis Presley), went from being among the poorest counties in the nation in the 1930s to a place of strong social capital and prosperity today. The business community united to invest in the dairy industry when King Cotton was on the decline. Today, Tupelo boasts a city foundation that awards more than a million dollars annually in grants to invest in infrastructure, the arts, education, and employee training. The North Mississippi Medical Center is the largest nonurban medical center in America. Seventeen Fortune 500 companies are located in Tupelo. Experts call this one of the top five community-development success stories in the nation.

One person can make a difference

The Tupelo story has many components, but perhaps its most inspiring aspect is that one person—George McLean, owner of the *Tupelo Journal* newspaper—rallied the business community to transform the town. McLean was liberal and idealistic. After he bought the *Journal* in 1934, he quickly antagonized the business community by his support (in print) of integration and striking textile workers, among other issues. But what he quickly learned was that while you need to "do the right thing . . . you can't lead without people following you."

So McLean tailored his message to the community, not by taking the moral high ground but by appealing to local self-interest. Amazingly, not long after they'd been locking horns, McLean was able to sell business leaders on the idea that if they pooled their money and invested in new ideas, everyone's prosperity would rise. Once that happened, according to Dr. Vaughn Grisham, Jr., a University of Mississippi professor of sociology who has made a life work of studying the "Tupelo turnaround," George McLean never let up.

McLean and others who joined with him worked to transform their community into a national model. Tirelessly, they worked to improve education and health care, to start the aforementioned foundation, and to invest in the arts and infrastructure. Once the business community realized the economic benefits of pulling together, it supported McLean and his progressive ideas and pushed for change.

You can change city hall

Most civic indicators in Portland, Oregon, jumped from the early 1970s to the present day as compared to comparable cities, in which civic engagement largely declined over that period. Why? In *Better Together*, Robert Putnam and Lewis Feldstein trace this change to a profound occurrence back in 1974. That year, neighborhood associations were incorporated into the formal governing structure of the city. When ninety neighborhood associations were invited to make official policy recommendations to any city agency on an array of matters, the community was successfully brought to the table. All of a sudden, instead of feeling themselves to be alienated outsiders, members of the general public were made to feel that they were stakeholders at the official table of community governance.

This feeling of enfranchisement has had a profound and lasting effect on citizens' connection to their community, as demonstrated by any number of social-capital benchmarks. Today, Portlanders write letters to the editor at a rate four times the national average. And fully 28 percent of Portlanders report that they served as officers of a local organization the previous year, compared to 7 percent elsewhere. Before 1974, these indicators in Portland were just average. The moral of this story is that when government opens its doors to the public, it has the power to transform a community and help its citizens build a more vital and vibrant future.

When evaluating your community—or a community to which you plan to move—it is wise to examine these factors. And once you've settled into a new community, do what you can to help boost citizen participation.

"Social capital impact statement"

Lewis Feldstein believes that social capital is so fundamental to the well-being of a community that when major decisions are being made about such things as schools, post offices, highway expansion, etc., that a new national indicator should be devised. He proposes calling it a "social capital impact statement." It would take into account how the given change would affect the social capital of an area. This statement wouldn't have to trump other considerations, he says. It would simply say that "when you are making a decision about whether to keep that post office open or not, or when you make that decision where to locate a school, take into account social capital. In New Hampshire, we are working with regional planning agencies to try and make this a regular part of the planning process."

on this Habitat house,' " Linda said. "And more than likely, they're going to choose working on a Habitat house because that becomes more fun than shopping. . . . But usually, they get so full of joy and they enjoy working on a Habitat house so much that they'll come back and back and back." She added jokingly that this can't-get-enough syndrome is often referred to as "Habitatitis."

A postcard of five beautiful Guatemalan children from my old college buddy and soul mate Liz Brody dated August 8, 1993, from El Rosario, Guatemala, is striking testimony to what Linda Fuller said. "This is near the Pacific Coast, mostly corn and cotton farmers," Lizzie wrote. "We are building homes for four families, and I have *never* had a better time in my life."

2. Gaining access to new sources of information

In a volunteer situation, you're interacting with the public, rubbing elbows with people in need. Think about it. Needy people are often the most resourceful folks you'll meet, because they have to be. You can pick up all kinds of new and useful information from them. And you may enjoy hearing the unvarnished truth. Sometimes, people who lack the calculating polish of the successful will tell you things that trained tongues might censure.

3. Entering new worlds

Millard Fuller, Linda's husband and the founder of Habitat, made a point to us when we all recently visited Holcomb's Hardware in Mount Airy. He said that volunteering stimulates—and stretches—the mind. "So many of us live in circles," Millard said. "If you are a member of the United Methodist Church, you live in the United Methodist circle. If you are a woman, you live in a woman's circle. If you are a Republican, you live in a Republican circle, and so on." But when you visit a Habitat for Humanity work site, "you get into other circles. You get out of an economic circle, and you get into a circle of people who are in a different economic level, and you get to realize that, 'wow, these people are very smart and are just as fully human as I am.' "

4. Finding a new direction

Mignon Turner, a twenty-one-year-old senior at Winston-Salem State University, credits volunteering with changing her life focus while in college. "When I started school, I was a mass communications major," she told me recently. "But after volunteering in the community and volunteering in Mexico as a study-abroad student, I realized I wanted to do international development and [international] affairs work."

Volunteering enables you to sample new areas and decide if you'd like to make a larger or longer commitment. And you don't have to be a student to look at new directions. Middle-aged and older people have found that volunteer experiences can be powerful and transformative.

5. Gaining new skills

Volunteering can help develop or enhance your skills in any number of arenas. When I worked as a volunteer board member for the United Fund of Greater Mount Airy for six years, I tried my hand at fund-raising. Fund-raising is usually viewed as an onerous task, something that few enjoy. While it wasn't a skill I sought out to learn, in trying my hand at it, I began to enjoy it. Fund-raising enables you to meet people you might not run across otherwise and to make a sales pitch for a worthy goal. It's amazing when people open their pocketbooks for a good cause. Skills learned in that context helped boost my fund-raising confidence level, which eventually led to a multiyear effort raising money for our television series on simple living. Sometimes, just trying on a new hat will help stretch you. And even if you never use that skill again, you will have enhanced appreciation for those who do.

Getting Started

If you've never before volunteered and want to give it a whirl, here are some ideas to help get you started:

1. Identify your interests

Identify a cause about which you feel passionately or at least strongly. You might start with something in which you or a close family member has a personal interest. For instance, a friend started raising money for cancer research after her daughter died of cervical cancer. I've known battered women who've emerged from that syndrome with a mission to help other women in need. If you have a passion for environmental stewardship or community beautification, start where your heart leads you.

Dennis Lowe, then director of the Best Friends program at the Surry Friends of Youth, once spoke to our Mount Airy Rotary Club about the need for caring adults to become "best friends" to needy youngsters. I signed up to be matched with a lively nine-year-old girl who lived with her father and sister in a trailer near the city. Once a week for a year, I spent an evening or afternoon with Trista, working on her homework or taking her out to eat or to a movie or a play. The high point of the year was accompanying Trista and other youngsters on a bus trip to Washington, D.C., to tour the capital and do an afternoon of volunteer work.

2. Create a niche

My friend Mary Woltz told me about her friend Howard, who has a unique volunteering niche: He enjoys helping people move. When Howard heard Mary was planning to move from Rockland County, New York, to Long Island, he called and offered to help pack, load the truck, unload, and get her settled. As Mary had always considered moving to be a pesky nuisance, she was floored by his generous offer. She gratefully accepted and learned something along the way. "Howard loves to help people move because, to him, it represents helping to launch them in a new part of their life—almost like a birthing," she told me. "Isn't that beautiful?"

3. Jump in

It takes no special credentials to become a volunteer. You don't need an organizational structure or an official program to do it. Think of an original idea and get going. Just post a notice on your church bulletin board, or ask around.

It could be planting trees. Just planting a few every season around your neighborhood will make a difference. Do you love washing cars? Maybe you'd like to help senior citizens get their cars washed. Just taking one person's car to the car wash every six weeks is a good deed that will make a big difference. Or it may be babysitting. My mother, Marie Whittaker, kindly watches her grandson Henry most every time we ask. But a less obvious candidate for the job—Edith McPeak, a senior citizen I met in the women's locker room at the local swimming pool—just volunteered to do it. She has since become one of Henry's—and our—favorite friends.

As a way to get started, Winston-Salem State University student Mignon Turner suggested calling organizations such as hospitals, churches, or school systems. "Even companies need volunteers," she said. Just call and ask how you can help, she suggested. If you're feeling blue during the holidays, this is an ideal time to offer an extra set of hands.

Volunteering has become an integral part of Mignon's life, and she draws on her strengths when she works. "Because I'm a Spanish major, I mainly work in school systems and dental offices, translating for students and adults there. But I also have a relationship with the Salvation Army Girls' Club." An honor student, Mignon helps youngsters with homework, arts and crafts, and organizational skills.

4. Treat the recipient of your service with respect

Never enter into volunteer work in a paternalistic or patronizing frame of mind. Go into any kind of service relationship with "a deep reciprocal sense . . . that the person you are in service with has just as much to give back as you have to give them," advises Campus Compact's John Saltmarsh. In order for the relationship to be meaningful and successful, "there has to be a deep respect for what that person's life experiences and knowledge is," he says.

5. Address local needs

Be sure to remember the profound but catchy call to action that's been popular now for several decades: "Think Globally; Act Locally." Though helping national campaigns and causes is worthwhile, the odds are great that you will have the most impact on projects right under your nose. If you're interested in water-quality issues, for example, look into the water needs in your community. Remember, when you volunteer locally, it's far easier to have an impact and also to monitor the outcome of your work.

There is no question that volunteering and community involvement can and will—if entered into in the right spirit—change your life. So get started. Even if you feel that your plate is already full and you couldn't possibly take on one new thing, try a page out of our book and take a baby step. If it goes no farther, that step is worthwhile in and of itself. But that baby step may also lead you down a new and invigorating life path, first walking, then galloping, then sprinting in a new direction.

CHAPTER 7

Good Health, Good Food

"Each moment, hour, day, week and year should be treated as an occasion—another opportunity to live as well as possible, in accordance with the old saying 'Tomorrow is a new day' or the new Mexican greeting 'Siempre mejor' (always better) in place of the conventional 'Buenos Dias' (good day). With body in health, emotions in balance, mind in tune and vision fixed on a better life and a better world, life, individually and collectively, is already better."

—Helen and Scott Nearing, in *Living the Good Life*

To peruse the magazine section of any bookstore these days, or to channel-surf the TV set, is to encounter a brave new religion in our culture. No, the religion is not sex, though sex is one of its prime sacraments. It's body worship—our absolute obsession with how our bodies look, and our tortured love-hate relationship with the food we put in them. We worship at the altar of the body, mortal though it may be. The body is now divine, and divinity is us.

I exaggerate only slightly. It would be interesting to quantify the total amount of time we devote, in one form or another, to indulging our bodies and our "body yearnings," particularly when we consider the time we spend chowing down, watching cooking shows, and talking about food.

This food (and diet) obsession is nothing to take lightly. Americans spend about $35 billion a year on weight-loss programs, yet nearly three-quarters of us remain overweight. As a nation, we have doubled the obesity rate—both for adults and children—in the last twenty years. By the end of this decade, more Americans are expected to die from obesity than from smoking. We eat, therefore we are—and for most of us, there's a lot of *are* to reckon with.

"The battle of the bulge," my mother, Miriam Levering, used to call that reckoning. Better to laugh than cry!

Underlying the cult of the body and its dark underbelly, the epidemic of obesity, is a pervasive yearning for better health—both physical and mental—and for improved eating habits. We know something's gone haywire, and we believe, with our American can-do pragmatism, that we will find our way to better overall health.

For all that, the national dialogue about health omits any significant linkage to a simpler life. True, when we talk about stress as a negative factor in health, we make vague references to the need to slow down. But we don't give serious thought to the big-picture connection between health and food issues and a simpler lifestyle. In neglecting that connection, we fail to see the forest for the trees. We miss a marvelous opportunity to make good health and good eating an integral part of daily life, not something we go out and acquire.

Where I grew up and still live—the Blue Ridge farming community of Orchard Gap—is not, and never was, Shangri-la. But the traditional lifestyle here is simple—hard physical work, yes, but along with it time to visit with neighbors, time to grow and prepare your own food, time to sit on the porch and "enjoy time," as the local expression has it. I know from lifelong observation that most neighbors older than I will live unusually long lives and remain physically fit deep into old age. They'll be fitter, I suspect, than many people half their age. Though congenitally averse to doctors, many of my neighbors treat non-life-threatening ailments with home remedies that seem to work in direct proportion to their faith in them.

What to make of this? I can only conclude from this anecdotal evidence that here is one case of a simpler lifestyle promoting health. Not that my frequently laconic neighbors make a big deal of it. They're simply living their lives the way they know how and relish—plenty of exercise, plenty of good eating, plenty of enjoying each other's company. In the older generation, at least—I worry about my Boomer generation, and younger ones, at Orchard Gap—simplicity and health are integrated naturally. Normal living is healthy living.

A thousand miles or more from Orchard Gap—but close, in many ways, in spirit—Helen and Scott Nearing also integrated simplicity and health. Their Harborside, Maine, farm was the last stop on two pilgrims' progress toward self-sufficiency. Wanda, a Mainer who met the Nearings in the mid-1970s at the World

Vegetarian Conference, which she covered as a teenage stringer for the *Bangor Daily News*, was one of the many beneficiaries of their mentoring.

The Nearings' quintessential philosophy was this: Live life close to its marrow. Whether in building your own house, growing and preparing your own food, or making your own music and providing your own entertainment, the Nearings defined the "good life," as they called it, as the direct, unmediated experience of natural rhythms and nature's bounty. Writing as fervently as they lived, they helped launch the back-to-the-land and simple-living movements. Their work continues to inspire new generations of readers. Healthy and strenuously active—both physically and mentally—for nearly their entire lives, Scott Nearing died at age one hundred and Helen at ninety.

There's much to be learned from them—and from my older neighbors in Orchard Gap. You don't have to be a homesteader or an Orchard Gap farmer to experience for yourself the health and culinary benefits of a simpler lifestyle. In cities and suburbs, where the vast majority of us live, there are many opportunities to integrate simplicity and health. With a little ingenuity, and perhaps to your surprise, you can make some of the same choices the Nearings did and apply the wisdom of family farmers to lives challenged not so much by weather as by choked freeways. What's needed most is an open mind. That, you already possess—or you wouldn't be reading these words!

Where You Live, Your Body Lives Also

"Geography," the saying goes, "is destiny." That may be stretching things a bit, but it's true that where we live can limit or expand our menu of choices. Life on a Blue Ridge farm jeopardizes considerably my prospects for regular dining at French restaurants! Life in New York City diminishes the possibility of encountering wild bears like the ones that wander into our cherry orchard. Geography is destiny.

Exercise, however, is possible just about anywhere. (Remember the astronauts jogging around their spaceship in the film *2001: A Space Odyssey?*) And few, if any, activities are more important for good health than exercise. Here are five major health benefits of regular exercise:

1. It helps keep weight under control

2. It improves cholesterol and blood pressure

3. It helps counter stress

4. It increases muscle strength and prevents bone loss

5. It helps delay or even prevent chronic illnesses and diseases associated with aging

How much exercise do we need to enjoy these and other benefits? Recommendations vary, but according to the Centers for Disease Control and Prevention, twenty minutes of daily walking per person could wipe out our obesity epidemic. Dr. Frank Spence, our physician friend in Elkin, North Carolina, reports that an hour a day of moderate exercise—or thirty minutes more than has been the norm—is the current recommendation from many professionals for overall good health. By reducing his work hours (see chapter 3), Frank has made time for his daily hour of exercise. So how do the rest of us break a sweat?

Traditionally, of course, we find the time to go to the gym, the health club, the "fitness center," the swimming pool, the walking path, or even the streets, for walking, jogging, or biking. In other words, we carve out from our time-pressed lives a sliver of time devoted exclusively to exercise—a sliver devoted to the body, much like the vaunted "quality time" time-starved workers carve out for family members.

There's nothing to sneeze about with this approach to exercise. Certainly, it does a body—if not necessarily the soul—good. And if, after careful examination, it's your only option, then by all means carve out that exercise sliver and do it. Few decisions could be worse in a time-challenged life than neglecting your body altogether. Lack of exercise alone, health professionals say, accounts for at least two hundred thousand deaths annually in the United States from heart disease, stroke, and diabetes.

There are two other positive approaches.

The first is Frank Spence's—a significant lifestyle change (in his case, a reduction of work hours) that allows for a wider margin in your life. An hour of exercise—usually, brisk walking on the streets of Elkin with his wife, Suzanne—fits comfortably into Frank's daily schedule. You reprioritize so that health comes first as part of a lifestyle that is itself less stressful.

"The Earth Gym"

The other positive approach is, as I see it, the most ingenious one. It's one we can learn from Scott and Helen Nearing (who were never known to devote time exclusively to exercise), from my neighbors (ditto), and from my brother-in-law Bill Van Hoy, now in his late eighties and still going strong. It's as simple as using "the earth gym," a clever New Age phrase for an old-fashioned idea: Exercise as you live, as you do those daily things that are necessary or good for you in themselves. The bottom-line trick here is to look for every opportunity—and I mean *every* one—to get some exercise.

One "earth gym" user I know is a commuter featured in the PBS film Wanda hosted, *Escape from Affluenza*. He lives in Seattle, and every day he commutes to work in his kayak. That's right, kayak. In Seattle, with its numerous waterways, it's possible for this hardy soul to kayak to work.

Most likely, a kayak commute is not on your options menu. But how about walking or biking to work?

Sure, if you live in Outer Mongolia and commute to downtown Megalopolis, USA, walking to work is not an option. But if you live a mile or two (or three) from work, what's wrong with hoofing it? When Wanda lived in New York City for two years working at the *Paris Review*, she walked a half-hour (or thirty-one blocks) to work each day from her apartment, then a half-hour back home. Nowadays, she frequently walks to business appointments from our Mount Airy office—another way (*during*, not before or after, the workday) to put walking to work for you.

If you can't hoof it, consider a bicycle. For years before he retired, my brother-in-law Charles Kern biked to work on Capitol Hill from his home in northwestern Washington, D.C., then biked home in the afternoon, getting all the exercise he needed on his daily commute. The morning ride invigorated him for the workday, helping him cope with the egos-on-parade of lobbyists and politicians! Gary Gardner, director of research at Worldwatch Institute, also in Washington, told us that he frequently commutes on his bike from across the Potomac in Virginia. Film and television actor Ed Begley, Jr., whose modest Studio City, California, home Wanda and I visited recently, reported that he regularly bikes to work when filming in Los Angeles, riding on trails across the Santa Monica Mountains or on "surface streets," as regular streets (as opposed to freeways) are known in L.A. Where there's a bike, there's a way.

Beyond the workplace, a walk up the stairs—as opposed to a ride in the elevator—to your apartment or anywhere else is a great way to get a quick workout. According to *Prevention* magazine, a recent study revealed that five two-minute "bouts of stairclimbing" offer the cardiovascular benefits of thirty-six minutes of walking.

Shopping at the mall? Instead of jostling for position to nail down that close-in parking space—and often idling in your car for God knows how long to get it—why not park on the fringe of the lot and take a walk? The obesity epidemic, I have a secret suspicion, can be traced directly to the perceived privilege of not having to walk anywhere!

"Simplify, simplify," Thoreau said. Like language teachers, he apparently believed in the power of repetition. Again, in the spirit of Thoreau, I say, "Walk, walk!" Scholars who study human evolution tell us that the body is built to be used actively, even strenuously. That's our evolutionary legacy. So shake a leg!

Don't like to walk uphill? That's not a problem if you live in Kansas—but if your name's not Dorothy, think again! Hills, which every farmer neighbor of mine deals with daily, are not public enemy number one for walkers. My father, Sam Levering, captain of the cross-country team at Cornell in the late 1920s, trained every summer on the steep hills flanking the family orchard. But you don't have to run up them! Fitness experts say that for every 5 percent of grade, brisk walkers burn off at least five calories per minute. Additionally, uphill walking builds strength and stamina.

The way to walk briskly up a hill? Lean forward slightly and use a larger-than-normal (but not exaggerated) arm swing. Bring your hips and buttocks into the action, making them help your thighs do the work. Question my credentials on this one? Believe me, in an orchard on the side of a mountain, I walk briskly uphill every day!

Yard Work

Yard work is the bane of warm-weather existence. To invest gobs of time in a yard and then thump our chests with pride in the results strikes me as folly worthy of Don Quixote's assaults on windmills—minus the nobility!

But if we must glorify our yards and our yard work—and keep the neighbors' righteous wrath at the sight of an unkempt yard at bay—why not get some health benefits from it? Enough of those decadent riding mowers and leaf blowers, which, like so many "convenient" and "time-saving" contraptions, give the lie to standard notions of "the good life." Stick with a push mower and a rake, which at least can break you into a sweat, as they do for me.

Think your yard's too big for a push mower and rake? Then your yard's too big. Period. Don't have the time to use a push mower and rake? Then your yard's too big. End of story. To have a yard—which, I concede, does offer one form of beauty, and a playground for children—only to roll over it on a riding mower, on your hind end, is to miss a terrific opportunity to burn some calories and enhance your health.

Flower and vegetable gardening are two additional earth-gym opportunities. Uprooting weeds, cutting native grasses, and planting new plants in her two flower gardens help keep our Santa Monica, California, friend Ellen Hoffs in trim shape in her sixties. For as long as I've known him—nearly forty years now—Bill Van

Hoy, my octogenarian brother-in-law, has tended a substantial vegetable garden outside his home in the North Carolina town of Asheboro. A retired high-school history teacher, grandfather, and now a widower (my sister Lois died in 1991), Bill can be seen most any warm-weather day right off U.S. 64. He's the man with the hoe. If there's any body fat on Bill "the Hoe" Van Hoy, only a microscope could find it. Rather than eat Bill's eggplants and such (which he will gladly give you upon request, whether you're a stranger or not), why not plant your own vegetable garden and pick up twin health benefits—fresh food, good exercise—in one activity? And by the way, a fine place for that new vegetable garden is that portion of your yard you got rid of so you could start using a push mower and a rake!

With all forms of earth-gym exercise, living in an environment conducive to exercise makes a real difference. Positive changes are often needed. Mixed zoning statutes where homes, offices, and stores mingle, making cities more walkable; constructing buildings where stairways are not hidden from view; building roads that accommodate bicyclists and pedestrians; creating better public-transportation systems to free up more road space for bicycle lanes—such changes would help enormously.

Still, opportunities to integrate exercise into daily activities exist everywhere, and it's all too easy to use suburban sprawl and other challenges as excuses for doing nothing. Resourcefulness and grit can overcome virtually anything.

Sleep Tight

It's no secret that stress undermines sleep. The fruits of contemporary, need-it-yesterday living—pressure, tension, anxiety—frequently ripen in the bedroom, away from the job and the home desk where the bills are piling up—but not really away from them. And when we sleep fewer hours than our body requires, we suffer not only short-term fatigue and a diminished quality of life but long-term health effects, too.

As I was growing up, my physically short but always feisty father, Sam, never relented in his "sleep eight good hours" health campaign, particularly when I brought night-owl habits acquired in college and grad school home for the holidays and summer work at the orchard. "Morning comes too soon," he'd always say, attempting to shove me to bed. Several physicians over the past twenty years have told me much the same thing—namely, that long-term sleep loss can diminish body function, particularly the ability to fight illness.

Becoming less stressed, then, is obviously good for your sleep and for your health. No rocket science there. It's common knowledge among folks who've simplified their lives that a simpler, more balanced life can reduce stress, relieve workplace and financial pressures, and reward you with the fulfillment of the familiar saying, "Now I can sleep at night."

A Nap a Day

But usually overlooked is the virtue of sleep that doesn't come at night. Will *your* employer allow you to take a nap? You'll never know if you don't ask. Tell that boss (if you have one) that even during World War II, Winston Churchill took regular afternoon naps. Every afternoon at four, Lyndon Johnson donned pajamas preparatory to his nap. According to Ralph Keyes in his book *Timelock*, other regular nappers included Harry Truman, Thomas Edison, Malcolm Forbes, and, in all likelihood, Ronald Reagan. In our society, with its macho work ethic, nappers of this sort might well be called "worknappers," folks who steal work productivity. But must we see it that way?

Humorously, Keyes notes the workplace sleight of hand of "resting our eyes" and other ways in which we "learn to doze without being obvious about it." He invokes General George Marshall, who "once observed that nobody ever had a good idea after 3 P.M." Research, Keyes suggests, bears out Marshall's comment: "Sleep experts now take it for granted that our body clocks are set to nap in the afternoon. . . . Among sleep researchers there is a near-consensus that naps increase alertness, raise energy levels, and improve mood. So far this finding has been virtually ignored in the world of work."

Who knows? In your workplace, maybe the powers that be will see a short nap for what it is: a blow for productivity.

In my workplace, I catch a nap almost daily. Working on this book, I've napped in midafternoon, thirty minutes at most, lying on the carpeted floor in my office and resting my head on a pillow. Coming out of the orchard, I, like my grandfather Ralph Levering, nap for half an hour after lunch. Grandfather Ralph did this religiously and, what's more, encouraged his work hands to do the same. Most of them did, at least in the warm-weather months, lying in the shade of the apple trees. Ahead of his time, Ralph was!

Keyes envisions a time in the workplace when "nap breaks will become as common as coffeebreaks. They're certainly better for you."

Let's hope he's right. In the meantime, if there's any way you can swing it, take an afternoon nap. If you're self-employed, then by all means try it! I can tell you from experience that, seen only from a work standpoint, naps generate productivity. Viewed in a larger context, they honor the body's natural rhythms, unleashing its energy according to nature's design. What could be simpler than taking a nap?

Live Outdoors All You Can

I was never a Boy Scout, but there's enough of the scouting philosophy in me to be a firm believer in the "at-home-ness" of our bodies in the great outdoors. Helen and Scott Nearing practiced a regimen of four hours a day outdoors. They theorized that the combination of physical exercise and New England sun and fresh air was as good a tonic as could be found anywhere. Though it's hard to argue with their results, few of us can duplicate the lives of the Nearings. We can, however, look for every opportunity to spend time outdoors, whether it's hiking in a nearby state park or even sitting on a porch taking in the evening air.

From a scientific standpoint, I suppose, linking outdoor exposure—protected by a hat and sunscreen, of course!—to better health is a tad dubious. But science doesn't always account for what we know in our bones. How do you quantify the effect on the body of sitting on a porch taking in a summer sunset? No doubt, such outdoor exposure isn't likely to cure bone cancer, if you happen to have that deadly disease. But over the long haul, I have no doubt that outdoor exposure contributes to good health. From an evolutionary perspective, it's where our bodies became our bodies and where, instinctively, they like to be.

The proof in the pudding—if any proof is needed—lies in our young son, Henry. Every chance we get, Wanda and I expose Henry to the simple delights of the outdoor world, whether it's the orchard or forest at home, a hiking trail, an ocean beach, or a city park. The health benefits for Henry, I'm absolutely convinced, go well beyond the exercise. In part, those health benefits may derive from the interplay of Henry's naturally imaginative mind with what the outdoors offers—a constantly changing and stimulating environment that engages all the senses.

This gut feeling of mine is the logic, if you will, of what is often called "holistic" thinking—the idea of mind-body interconnection. More specifically, this holistic view has it that the condition of our mind directly impacts our health. "The greatest force in the human body," author Norman Cousins writes, "is the natural drive of the body to heal itself—but that force is not independent of the belief system, which can translate expectations into physiological change."

Simple translation: Healthy mind equals healthy body. For most people—and certainly young Henry—outdoor exposure refreshes and invigorates the mind. If you can't keep pace with the Nearings, then at least take every opportunity you have to be outdoors!

Practice the Art of Massage

The holistic mind-body approach can apply also to the effects of massage. Most of us have had the massage experience in one form or another, both on the giving and receiving ends. What we've learned is that a good massage is a great de-stresser, that body and mind relax as one system. What most of us have also learned is that we'd like to have a lot more of them! Consider this question, asked only half in jest: Is a time-starved life without a daily massage (or two) a life really worth living?

If you have a significant other, the art of massage can be very significant indeed! One of the great things about massages is that you don't have to be a professional masseuse to give them to a loved one. And like most good things, they cost nothing! On the other hand, getting a little instruction from a pro—as in a one-day workshop—can increase your skill and make a great Valentine's Day (or any other day) gift to your partner.

Workshops teach basic techniques effective in loosening the knots that often appear around the base of the skull, associated with tension headaches. They also provide instruction in relaxing and limbering the back, shoulders, arms, legs, and feet. A good massage workshop enhances your overall understanding of your body's structure and functions.

The ice is a tad thin here, but why limit massages to your partner? With anyone you love, a massage is a beautiful gift. Consider it an expression of altruistic love. My late sister Lois—wife of Bill "the Hoe" Van Hoy—used to massage my back and shoulders in a way to die for. The lasting effects may have left my body, but her expressions of love will linger in memory as long as I live.

Limit Tube Time

Beware of that TV set! Now, there's a health tip from left field. After all, mind rot is the major health issue with television, right? Studies on the effects of television viewing have focused primarily on television's effects on the mind—particularly violent behavior in response to programs depicting violence. But does television viewing also affect our physical health?

Call it the Couch Potato Syndrome. Television, arguably the most seductive medium ever invented, can help make you fat. Recent studies confirm what might seem self-evident: The more people watch TV, the less they exercise, the more they eat in front of the tube, and the more they tend to weigh. This is true of children as well as adults. The studies also suggest that kids with TVs in their bedrooms are more likely to be overweight.

How to watch less TV? It seems like a silly question—just turn it off! My brother and sister-in-law, Ralph and Patty Levering, faced that question as they raised their two sons, Matthew and Brooks, now grown. Their solution was to place their one and only TV set in their relatively uninviting basement. Brilliant!—or so it seems to me. One of the reasons we watch too much television is the electronic-hearth factor. By this I mean putting a TV set in an emotionally warm, nestlike setting, the place where—particularly in the cold-weather months—we most want to be in our home. Making a television the focal point of an inviting room—particularly creating one of the entertainment-center-dominated rooms so popular nowadays—is fairly asking for TV addiction. Add the meals and snacks consumed while watching the set and a remote control that allows you to become one with your couch, and look out! Obesity, here you come.

Food for Thought

Every family I've ever met has a culinary history, a storehouse of family traditions and memories revolving around food. Think about your own family. Filed away in your memory bank are thousands of sense images—tastes, scents, textures, scenes from the kitchen and dining-room tables, the way a skillet full of sliced apples sounded as your grandmother fried them up. The memory bank goes on and on. Combine your memories with those of your relatives and you have a large fraction of what we mean when we talk about family—a group of people who've broken bread together time and again, who share a common experience and work together toward common goals.

Simplicity is at the heart of a healthy relationship with food. When we sit down and eat a good meal in fellowship with others, the pleasures are simple: flavorful food, good company, and the experience, rare these days, of the value of time for its own sake. Likely, we tell stories that transport us to earlier days. If we are members of a family, we participate, consciously or unconsciously, in long culinary traditions and in the implied values of those traditions.

Three generations of Leverings who've farmed the same orchard and lived on it since 1908 make for a distinctive culinary history. Though fruit—particularly apples, peaches, and cherries—is the centerpiece of that history, each family member across those three generations has been known for his or her singular, sometimes eccentric, tastes in food.

Everyone who knew him recalls my grandfather Ralph's love of the cream he extracted from the milk of his own cows. He'd ladle that cream on fresh fruit—and just about everything else! In his older years, my father, Sam, ground up raw wheat and soybeans in the woodshed, cooked the mixture in a double boiler, added homemade applesauce and powdered milk, and ate the final product at least two meals a day. What my mother viewed as a healthy eccentricity my father saw as delectable and wholesome dining! Miriam, my mother, was famous throughout the area for her fruit compote, a mixture of sliced fruits from the orchard steeped in the fruits' own juices, frozen, then removed from the freezer and served as it was thawing, often still studded with ice crystals but always with the juice beginning to run. Oh, my, was that compote out of this world!

The thread that runs through these three tidbits from my family's culinary history is time—the time it took for my grandfather to win his prized cream from the milk of his cows; for my father to grind and cook up his wheat and soybeans and to grow his apples and make the applesauce; for my mother to peel and core and seed and slice fruit, then mix it all up in kettles, ladle it into little boxes, put it in the freezer, and break out those boxes and thaw them. *Time*. Time spent with food at or near its source, time devoted to the dual purposes of eating and communing.

That's simple living the old-fashioned way. But those three people, and most everyone else in their generations, have faded from the orchard scene, never to appear among those trees again, except in the half-light of memory. As for my generation and the generation following mine, do we take time to eat well, to connect food in any meaningful way with our lives and with the earth? Do we even *have* the time to make those connections?

As producers of food who make the bulk of our living selling what we grow, Wanda and I of necessity are sensitive to public perceptions about food and the latest food trends. We keep abreast of what's being written and said about food, particularly fruits and vegetables. Every fruit season at our pick-your-own operation, we have the chance to talk face to face with thousands of fruit consumers. In addition, through our community involvement and business activities, we know dozens of farmers and agricultural professionals—extension agents, college professors, marketers—around the country, people who also have their ears to the ground about the numerous food issues that—particularly since the Alar chemical scare with apples—now swirl through the minds of many consumers as they make point-of-purchase decisions and feed themselves and their families.

Time itself has become issue number one. Do we take time to eat well, to eat thoughtfully? Many of us don't. So the issue—*the* issue—for many Americans about food is simply the lack of time. Into the breach jump the much-vilified McDonald's and a dizzying array of fast-food and grocery-store alternatives to home-grown and home-cooked food. Prepackaged, microwaveable meals and eating out have arrived to save us from our time starvation. In fact, Americans—once justifiably proud of our regional cuisines and our ability to showcase them in our homes—now spend more money on restaurant food than we do on the food we cook ourselves.

A second major issue can best be summarized by the following question: What's *in* our food? For many people, this question inspires several others. Is the food nutritious? Is it high in cholesterol and fat, or is it "heart-healthy"? How was it grown and/or processed? Were chemicals used, and are those chemicals in the food? What other things were used—what resources, for example—that are a part of the story of this food?

Food, we all know, is fundamental. Without it, we would die. Reports by young urban schoolchildren that food is made in supermarkets notwithstanding, the ways that it was grown and delivered to your table have environmental consequences. Indeed, there's nothing quite like food to connect us to the earth, to the rhythm of the seasons and the life cycle of plants and animals. If all the world's a stage, as Shakespeare said, then all the world's also a farm. And buying and consuming food inevitably makes environmental actors of us all.

Food makes a journey to your table. Increasingly, consumers are asking, "How green was that journey?" All food—like the favorite foods of my parents and grand-father—has a story. But when we try to make thoughtful, informed food decisions—simple decisions that make sense personally, for the good of our society, and for the environment—the story can seem complex.

There's a good reason for that: It *is* complex. There's a lot at stake here—not only big money and controversial new developments like genetically modified crops, but also ideology and the moral high ground. "Spin" comes brazenly from all directions—from agribusiness and food conglomerates on one extreme to organic-food-only advocates on the other to everything in between.

For the average food consumer—whoever that may be—who wants to do the right thing without deifying food as the Meaning of Life, in every direction are "spun" images of food perfection. Organic food, it seems, originates in some blissful, verdant valley where bunnies hop and birdies sing. Ingesting that morally correct carrot will increase your virtue quotient by at least 75 percent. You'll feel so, so good about yourself! Or McDonald's burgers and cereals from General Mills will increase family togetherness and contentment by 80 percent at least. And Ronald McDonald truly is a wonderful role model for your child.

What to make of these various pictures? How do we lift the veil of consumer manipulation and know what to do?

Here are a few things to think about and some options to weigh as you try to simplify your food stream and enhance your dining experience.

Eat More Meals at Your Dining Table

Let's start with this most basic of basic strategies. A generation ago, who would have needed to be invited to eat more meals at their own dining table? Nowadays, though, it's the rarest of luxuries. Here are two reasons to do it:

1. Eating with family or friends at your own dining table is a bonding experience par excellence. Even when everyone's tired or "not in the mood," sitting down and sharing time and food with loved ones signals that you really do share their world and they yours. What better way to acknowledge and reinforce that idea?

Having originated in Italy in reaction to the invasion of a McDonald's franchise, the "slow food" movement has taken hold in a number of American cities, notably New Orleans, where Wanda and I ate gumbo with Poppy Tooker and her slow-food group recently. The slow-food concept was founded on the idea that time spent preparing food and then dining with friends in your or someone else's home celebrates food's origins, the labor (and, with luck, the love) involved in growing it, and its overall cultural worth.

It's an idea worth applying in our own homes. True, few people these days can sit down with family or friends three meals a day. But we can find time to do it occasionally. If you can't find the time, *make the time*—it's that important. Schedule regular "sit-downs" if you can—Wednesday night? Sunday lunch?—and stick to them.

2. Food is better if you've taken time to prepare it yourself. With inventive cooks, at any rate, there's nothing like a home-cooked meal. And if more people than the cook hang out in the kitchen, or if more people than one do the cooking, the pleasure of fellowship seems to linger in the taste of that food at the table!

Cook in Bulk and Use a Freezer

One of the simplest tricks for cutting down on overall cooking time (if that's what you sometimes need to do) is to cook in bulk. It's easy. Make a big pot or two of something you just love to eat. Our two favorites are pasta sauce (plenty of garlic, olive oil, and a medley of chopped vegetables and tofu) and what I call my "First Grub, Then Ethics Stew" (from a phrase of German playwright Bertolt Brecht), which is not actually a stew but a simmered mix of rice, tofu, vegetables, and salsa, again heavy on the garlic and olive oil. If you have a freezer (where you can also keep a lot of other things—frozen fruits and vegetables, etc.), the genius of this scheme is that, after that first meal straight from the big pot, you've got a slew of meals already essentially prepared. And the freezer, at least according to my taste buds, doesn't diminish the original flavor at all.

Grow Your Own Food

Really want to get down and dirty with Mother Earth? There's nothing like growing vegetables and fruits yourself. Like preparing your own meals, it's a time-hog, perhaps the major reason why vegetables gardens are an endangered species, even among folks who have an ample plot in which to plant them. But the rewards—including exercise, as mentioned earlier—are well worth it.

For the past several years, Henry and I have been our primary vegetable gardeners, an A-1 father-son bonding experience, just as it was for my father and me. Our modest enterprise of growing tomatoes, lettuce, radishes, squash, corn, and green beans pales in comparison with most of our neighbors' and many of our fruit customers' vegetable gardens—but we'll take it. Henry's learning the same lessons I did growing up: Food doesn't grow in cans and jars, and it takes a little effort to be food's nursemaid.

There's no reason an urban environment should deter you. City dwellers are discovering that even a small patio filled with heirloom tomato plants can yield a large satisfaction, as it does for Laura Fletcher, an ER physician we met recently at her Los Angeles apartment. Suburban and small-town vegetable gardening is a cinch. If there's a yard, there's a way. If you have a back lot, so much the better.

Backyard orchards are a tad more challenging, but again, your prospects are generally good. Los Angeles actor Ed Begley, Jr., prides himself on his roughly twenty-by-twenty backyard (actually, front-yard) orchard, which includes dwarf apple and citrus trees. With visions of plucking backyard cherries and other fruits dancing in their heads, many of our customers grill me for advice on what varieties to plant and how to tend the trees.

Most good libraries have books on how to grow your own fruit. One of my most basic tips is to know your climate well—even the microclimate of your backyard. Since fruit buds and blossoms are unusually vulnerable to late-winter and spring cold, the hardiness of the fruit and its many varieties, the bloom dates of varieties in your location, and the likely air temperatures at your site may well determine whether your crop will survive a freeze.

Eat Lower on the Food Chain

If you're a practicing carnivore, do you ever feel a twinge as you devour that slice of cow, chicken, or other meat? Perhaps not. But many people do these days, and quite a few of the Twingers—a nod to the Quakers, so called because they were accused of "quaking" in the presence of the divine!—are giving up meat altogether. Not all folks eschewing meat are so-called activist eaters—that is, people who take political, ethical, and monetary issues into account when they buy and prepare foods. But most vegetarians are keenly aware of the environmental impact of meat production and consumption. They're also aware of the well-documented brutalities and sanitation practices of many forms of livestock production and slaughter, none worse than in the industrial chicken "farms," where savage practices you don't want to know about as you're cruising the drive-thru at KFC take place with scarcely a murmur from the carnivorous public.

Not everyone is quite as categorical as Helen Nearing, who wrote in *Simple Food for the Good Life*, "We cannot eat flesh without unkindness and violence and cruelty." But it is hard to disagree with one of our most celebrated vegetarians (she was not, by the way, a vegan) when she went on to say, "All diets are relative to the consciences of the eater. One cannot be perfectly consistent in living, but a more or less harmless way of life is possible, and if not as pure as the purest one can at least try to be not as gross as the grossest."

From the standpoint of land use and feed waste, the case against meat is unsparingly clear. According to the Worldwatch Institute, "a calorie of beef, pork, or poultry needs 11 to 17 calories of feed," and "95 percent of soybean harvest is eaten by animals, not people." By eating these foods directly—eating lower on the food chain—we humans open the door to vastly more efficient use of land and, particularly in the case of industrial-style pig and cattle production, less pollution of soil, water, and air. According to Worldwatch, "producing 8 ounces of beef requires 25,000 liters of water." Agriculture in general "accounts for 70 percent of world water use." With water shortages approaching crisis status in many regions, beef production and consumption can seem wasteful, even environmentally irresponsible.

These issues can be wrenchingly complex, both personally and on a societal, even planetary, scale. Though I'm a vegetarian at home and in restaurants, I'm not when I'm served meat by a generous host who's taken the time and trouble to prepare a dish she or he takes great pride in and who doesn't know—usually through my own negligence—my proclivities. Perhaps you would make a different choice—a "purer" choice.

By the same token, one of my closest friends—a farmer who lives nearby—raises beef cows for a living. While it's all very well to inveigh against beef production—criticism that almost always comes from people who have never had to farm—my friend is a community pillar who's done more for our rural county and region, across a spectrum of socially and economically beneficial activities, than two hundred of his fellow citizens. He's also raising beef organically and quite consciously doing the least possible environmental harm he can. Here, it seems to me, as we do with a variety of tough social and economic issues, we have to weigh both the upside and the downside of activities.

We should be extremely judicious both as consumers and as critics of mainstream agriculture. There is, unfortunately, a reason for the stark fact that most American farmers feel estranged from environmental activists. Many environmentalists look only at the issue they care about most. Alas, this is also true of many farmers, for whom that issue is the bottom line of financial survival. While environmental issues have never been more critical, and while the sometimes self-serving resistance of farmers and agribusiness in general to environmental progress does little to help solve our mutual problems, it's also true that no problems will be solved by blanket calls for change that fail to address economic issues and put a human face on economics. The results can only be polarization and stalemate.

Jesus, of all beings, seems relevant to me as we face the practical realities of progressive change. No professing Christian I've ever known—including my highly idealistic parents—ever came close to actually living the unnervingly radical Christian ideal as Jesus proposed it. The bar is just too high. But it's an inspiring ideal that compels many people to be more compassionate, more forgiving, more tolerant than they might otherwise be.

That, it seems to me, is one useful analogy when we think about consuming meat. Know the facts, and set a high bar. But neither hold yourself above your fellows nor berate yourself for understandable inconsistencies. "All diets," as Helen Nearing said, "are relative to the consciences of the eaters." And we cannot, as Nearing conceded, "be perfectly consistent in living." The frequent fuel-guzzling airplane trips of high-profile environmental activists underscore the point.

The best course of action, I believe, is to examine your conscience, weigh all the factors, and aim as high as you can in the context of your life. Here's a modest proposal (not to be confused with Jonathan Swift's "Modest Proposal" to eliminate poverty by eating the poor!): Eat less meat than you are eating now. Cut it down by half or more. That gesture alone will make a positive difference. Over time, if you are so led, move toward "compassionate vegetarianism"—vegetarianism that is compassionate to all.

And if you're a vegetarian or a vegan already? You're eating the healthiest diet possible, both environmentally and for your body. You're eating closer to the millions of people in poorer countries who count themselves lucky to consume *any* of those grains we pass on up the chain. And you're eating *richly*.

Recently, in her Cambridge, Massachusetts, apartment, Frances Moore Lappé, author of the three-million-copy treatise on the world's food supply, *Diet for a Small Planet*, described to us the early days of her conversion from "the meat loaf, mashed potatoes, and frozen peas" diet of her Fort Worth, Texas, upbringing. "Rather than thinking of a plant-centered diet as some kind of deprivation, it was the opposite. It was just this wondrous world of variety and excitement . . . all the varieties of grains, all the varieties of nuts and seeds, all the varieties of peas and beans and lentils. We are talking about dozens and dozens and dozens. And the colors and textures and the tastes and the aromas!"

A handsome, slender woman now in her late fifties, Lappé found in her new diet a way to feel comfortable about the food entering her body. "I was a compulsive eater. I've never been fat, but I've always had those extra pounds that you know you always want to lose—until I started this way of eating. And then for thirty-something years, I've never had to ever count calories, ever weigh myself. Because now they are understanding more why that is. When we eat whole foods . . . your tastes align with what your body weight calls for, so that you are not battling with food anymore. And I think that was another piece of the pleasure because I'd always seen food like many Americans, particularly American women. You know, food as a threat. It is going to put on pounds. And so it is always this tug of war. And I let go. And it wasn't even an effort to let go—it just happened!"

Lappé believes that choosing a plant-centered, whole-foods diet is the perfect starting point for people wanting to simplify their lives. "The reason I think that it works for many people as a starting point," she told us, "is, yes, because we choose food every day. But also I think it is empowering to know that you are consciously not a victim of advertising. You are shopping with your own consciousness about what is good for you. . . . You start with the food question and then you say, 'Wait a minute. What other choices can I be making that make me feel more aligned and therefore more powerful?' "

But What About Pesticides?

What about them indeed? Of all the questions we're asked at the orchard, "Do you use pesticides?" ranks second in frequency only to "How do you keep the birds out of your cherries?" (Answer: We don't. The birds—which arrive in droves—gobble their fair share.)

In theory, I'm all for organic agriculture—or "sustainable" agriculture, as advocates call it. In a perfect world—where, in addition to everyone being a vegetarian or vegan, all cattle farmers would have great livelihoods in other professions—we'd grow and consume only organic food. There's no question that certain pesticides that have "long life" are not good for the environment. Nor are they good for the farmers or farm workers who apply them, particularly if they are used carelessly. Nor are they good for food consumers. To what degree pesticides harm consumers is a matter of debate. Generally speaking, the data remains sketchy, and figures are bandied about along both sides of the ideological divide.

We do use pesticides at our orchard. More specifically, I use them. I am the person who mixes them into a five-hundred-gallon water tank, then sprays them onto the fruit trees from an air-blast sprayer drawn, precariously at times, along steep hillsides by a four-wheel-drive tractor. It's scary work not so much because of the pesticides (I don't use the real killer-dillers) but because a mistake with two thousand pounds behind me, headed down a steep hillside, could easily lead to a fatal accident. More farmers are killed annually, on a percentage basis, than workers in any other profession. One of my predecessors in this job—while I still lived and worked in California—turned over both tractor and air-blast sprayer and is alive only by the grace of the Almighty.

I draw this picture to make a point: Many farmers take enormous risks not only with their fragile crops but with their lives. As a matter of course, we do risk assessments. As any good Western hero would, we tend to view the world as a place where a certain degree of risk is necessary, even beneficial. Without risk, what is ever gained?

But is it too risky for a society to live with pesticides in its food supply?

Ask the EPA—whether under Democratic or more lenient Republican tenure—and the answer is no. The politically sensitive EPA makes a broad-side-of-a-barn target for environmental activists, and criticism of its decisions about pesticides is not entirely unjustified. Still, the EPA has in the past few years phased out a number of the more controversial pesticides and has a reputation among fair-minded observers for ultimately erring on the side of consumer safety—perhaps not in every case, but in general.

Such fair-mindedness was nowhere in evidence on the CBS "gotcha!" program *60 Minutes*—and in certain environmental advocacy organizations—when Alar was portrayed to the American public as a dangerous chemical compound when applied to apples. Alar, as it turned out, was no such thing. But the economic effects on Washington State apple growers were pretty nearly deadly. Many on-the-bubble growers went under, and many more hung on for dear life. Though we'd long since discontinued the use of Alar on the apples at our farm, we watched the media feeding frenzy in dismay. Our own customers, understandably, asked leading questions. Simply put, they and millions of other apple lovers had been led down a less-than-appetizing primrose path.

Are pesticides, then, too risky in your personal food supply? Perhaps only you—not CBS, not the food producers, not the strict prohibitionists—should make that decision. I do think, though, that it's advisable to make the sort of risk assessment that farmers must make every day. Do the well-established health benefits of fruits and vegetables—which exist in "sprayed" produce as well as in organic produce—outweigh the risks of ingesting pesticide residues?

Weighing the Risks

In a recent conversation in Cambridge, Massachusetts, Jim Hammitt, Wanda's college classmate and now a professor at the Harvard School of Public Health, put the matter this way: "We have a tendency to focus too much on small risks and ignore some bigger risks. . . . The field of risk perception is interesting because most of us tend to focus on some particular aspect of an issue or a risk. So pesticides in your food, if you think about it, cannot be good because pesticides are there to kill pests. They are toxic, so why would you want them on your food? But if you look a little bit more carefully, often very, very little amounts of pesticides remain on the food at the time when they are eaten."

In other words, there are big risks, and there are small risks. Keep your perspective. And as Hammitt went on to advise concerning any activity affecting your health, examine the evidence and weigh the risks versus the benefits. True, with food, you could avoid this altogether simply by buying organic only. But as a practical matter, what if, overnight, we all did that? What would likely happen if all pesticides were abruptly banned and American farmers were required to grow organically or not grow at all?

There are those who would debate me on this point, citing studies indicating that, over time, yields from organically grown crops equal—or nearly equal—nonorganic yields. But given the economic realities of our current food system, American food production would in all likelihood decrease sharply for an indeterminate length of time as the shakeout occurred. For who knows how long, the economic effects on farming regions would be devastating, as many farmers would either go out of business or struggle to reinvent their way of farming in environments not always hospitable to organic production.

Meanwhile, consumers—many of whom, on tight budgets, currently can't afford organic food—would be forced to rely heavily on food grown offshore, where pesticide residue standards typically fall short of our own. In all likelihood, the net effect would be that consumers would eat far fewer, say, apples than they do now, as it would be exceedingly difficult to grow commercially acceptable organic apples in quantities that would feed our population. Both for individuals and for our society, would eating fewer apples be healthier than eating more apples treated with pesticides?

In the long run, it's clear that sustainable agriculture is the right idea. But how, as a practical matter, do we get there?

We get there thoughtfully, I think, and by degrees. Like Jim Hammitt, we keep our heads when it comes to pesticides; we learn, as soon as we can, the techniques for making the transition; we offer financial incentives to farmers to grow organically; we educate consumers not only about the virtues of organic production but also that "cosmetically challenged" food tastes just as good; and ultimately, we let market forces take us where we need to go. Organic farming is well worthy of support. Let's get there as quickly as we can. But let's not abandon in a headlong rush the major source of our food.

Many farmers are in transition already. At our orchard, though we still use pesticides when absolutely necessary—cherry production on a viable commercial scale is positively impossible in our wet climate without fungicides—we rely on natural predators as much as possible, following techniques known as "integrated pest-control management." In the past fifteen years, we've cut our pesticide use roughly in half, and the chemicals we use are generally less toxic than those used previously. And we're not alone.

How should all this impact your food decisions at this moment? The answer will depend on your values and your risk assessment. It may also depend on other factors—such as the one we'll consider next.

Buy Locally Grown Food

Given a choice, should you buy locally grown food? And consider this: Given a choice between locally grown food on which pesticides have been used and organically grown food that has been shipped a great distance, with all the attendant pollution and energy-use issues, which should you buy?

Consider our cherries. Your choice should be easy—if you live near our orchard. Surely, you'll buy our locally grown cherries, which are fresher and riper than similarly grown Washington State cherries in the supermarket, and which have not been shipped in tractor-trailers all the way across the country, which causes pollution and wastes energy. But what about organically grown cherries? There they are at the health-food store—not cheap by a long shot, but mighty tempting. Still, they've been shipped a long way, which means a lot of fossil fuel has been burnt and a lot of contaminants have been used in keeping them chilled.

So you'll come to my place? But the cherries you'll buy from me were personally sprayed by me! What's a virtuous health nut to do?

Surprise! If I were that health nut, I'd buy those local cherries. In buying locally grown food, you help alleviate some major problems in our food system—that is, the system encompassing the production, processing, marketing, transportation, packaging, preparation, consuming, and waste management of our food.

Here's the big picture: Produce grown in the United States typically travels fifteen hundred to twenty-four hundred miles from farm to plate. Whereas locally grown produce is usually sold within twenty-four hours of harvest, produce shipped from distant states or from foreign countries can spend from one to two weeks in transit. Along with fast food, we now have long-distance food, which, in addition to burning fossil fuel and pumping carbon emissions into the atmosphere severs food consumers from the source of their food supply.

Consider this: Do you feel any real connection to that head of lettuce you just bought in your grocery store? Why should you? A head of lettuce shipped from Salinas, California, to Washington, D.C., requires three times as much fossil-fuel energy in transport as it provides in food energy at its destination. Meanwhile, unable to cope with the economics of long-distance food production, family farmers are replaced by corporate farms, depriving virtually every region of our country of the culturally and often environmentally stabilizing influence of farmers invested in the nurture of land they own. Since 1937, the United States has lost 4.7 million farms, and fewer than a million Americans now describe themselves primarily as farmers. Thomas Jefferson, remember, said that farmers form the essential core of our democratic society.

In addition to buying superior ripeness, taste, and freshness, your purchase of locally grown food keeps dollars circulating in your community. (Eighteen cents of every dollar for produce bought at large supermarkets goes to growers and eighty-two cents to middlemen.) This is good for the farmer, for the merchants he supports, for the workers he hires, and for the preservation of his land in the face of development that is gobbling up forty-six acres of American farmland every hour.

Buying locally produced food also gives you a chance to influence the quality of farm production, introducing you to neighbors who may indeed be responsive to your needs and requests. If they aren't, they won't be in business for long! At farmers' markets and pick-your-own farms like ours, you can talk directly with food producers, ask questions, find out how and why things are done the way they are, suggest alternatives, and—ultimately—vote with your dollars.

Perhaps best of all, buying locally grown food links community members to one another, builds trust and mutual support, and increases overall knowledge about food and the "foodshed" of your area—a term that refers to the flow of food from where it's grown to where it's consumed. Making your personal foodshed as local as possible can positively impact local food production and values for years to come.

CSA's

These days, one of your best options for buying locally grown food is joining a CSA (Community Supported Agriculture) farm. CSA's are sprouting up all over the country, fueled by consumer hunger for fresh food and for direct contact with farmers. Likely, there are CSA's not far from you. Though we're not members, young Henry—then five—and I spent an afternoon a year ago with a group of

CSA farmers and curious potential customers near Floyd, Virginia, about an hour's drive from our orchard. Invited by our friend Tenley Weaver, an organic vegetable grower who also buys and sells our fruit at the Blacksburg, Virginia, farmers' market, Henry and I were ready to hear the CSA sales pitch.

We weren't disappointed. Among the group was Polly Heiser, one of the operators of Seven Springs Farm near Floyd, a CSA farm since 1991. Like other CSA farms, Seven Springs offers consumers a seasonal share in what it grows, delivering to its members twice a week a variety of organically grown vegetables.

"What we think is good," Polly told the group, "is that our members share the risk with the farmer. It doesn't make sense for the farmer to take all the risks. If there's no crop, the member is in the same boat as the farmer. If there's a bumper crop, the member gets a lot extra. At the same time, you're building relationships, building community, around food. It's more fun this way for everybody. Besides that, the food tastes better, and local food is more nutritious, therefore more satisfying. The shipped-in food, because it's not as nutritious, you eat more of it."

Though it was the dead of winter and we didn't get to see or taste anything grown "in season," Wanda and I had a chance to visit the headquarters of The Food Project, a CSA farm for suburban Boston customers that also sells produce at farmers' markets in low-income neighborhoods like Roxbury, the Boston neighborhood where the project is based.

"Creating personal and social change through sustainable agriculture," the organization's slogan goes. The stories we heard from two teenage boys about their growth while working with The Food Project appear to substantiate the claim. Every summer on its twenty-one-acre farm outside Boston and on two inner-city Roxbury lots, hundreds of Boston-area teenagers—some of them from homeless shelters—become organic farmers and marketers under the mentorship of adults.

The results? Annually, two hundred thousand pounds or more of corn, raspberries, carrots, rutabagas, and other crops are harvested and either sold or donated to homeless shelters. And character is built—one of the primary missions of the organization, along with teaching farming and marketing skills. "Small farms," said Patricia Donahue Gray, The Food Project's executive director, "are so economically challenged that they are going out of existence. Luckily, there are some new young people who are interested in taking up farming."

Young people taking up farming? Now, there's some good news! And the good news also is that there are customers out there ready and eager to buy what they grow!

When You Can, Drink Tap Water

Our longtime friend Pat Woltz, now in her seventies, is the sort of person who dispenses good advice no matter the subject, yet always unobtrusively and with a wonderfully light touch. When I was in high school in Mount Airy, Pat's son Howell was one of my best friends, and the friendship often carried me to Pat's house. There, I found wisdom as needed, on everything from nutrition to good authors. (Thomas Wolfe, Pat advised, was an excellent choice, particularly for a young, aspiring writer!)

Back home in Mount Airy after my own Wolfeian journeys elsewhere—yes, Thomas, you can go home again!—I continue to listen carefully when Pat speaks. Recently, in her kitchen, she told Wanda and me that she drinks "filtered" water. "It's simple to do," Pat said. She explained that she and her environmentalist daughter, Mary, a frequent visitor, decided to scrap their bottled water and its plastic jugs in favor of more eco-friendly refreshment.

Entering Pat's house from her well, the water she drinks is first distilled—boiled to vapor, then cooled and condensed to potable liquid—and then filtered with a charcoal filter. The system, Pat told us, is relatively inexpensive to set up and economical to operate, soon paying for itself when compared with never-ending water jugs. Pat's happy, Mary's happy, and maybe even the water is happy. End of story.

According to the Worldwatch Institute's *State of the World* report, the story of the widespread popularity of bottled water does not have such a happy ending. Our beverage of choice these days—worldwide, we spend an estimated $35 billion for it annually—bottled water comes at a steep environmental price. In addition to the fossil fuel use in transporting bottled water, the pollution from plastic production, and the issue of plastic waste (in 2002, Americans bought roughly 14 billion water bottles, 90 percent of which were thrown away), a lot of water in an increasingly water-depleted world is required to produce the plastic bottles. To make a single kilogram of the plastic most commonly used in water bottles, 17.5 kilograms of water are required.

When seen from this vantage point, Pat Woltz's filtered-water system seems even more desirable. As *State of the World* notes, "Given the environmental impacts of the use and disposal of bottled water, it is worth asking if there is not a better way to distribute this vital resource. For those of us fortunate enough to have the option, tap water (filtered, if necessary) is the cheaper, less polluting choice."

Develop a Philosophy That Works for You

Really want to simplify your diet? Helen Nearing had the answer, albeit in a somewhat politically incorrect way. "One way to reduce the housewife's work by half," she wrote in her delightfully curmudgeonly *Simple Food for the Good Life*, published in 1980, "is to make raw foods a major part of the diet, or eat raw foods entirely."

Most of us won't go that far, despite Nearing's contention that raw foods are "living foods—sunlight foods . . . with no extensive gap between the life-giving forces of the plant and the living forces of our bodies." But we might want to consider her advice that we should eat at least one raw food at every meal, particularly if we subscribe to her notion that "cooked or canned or frozen foods are embalmed, dead foods. . . . Cooking is killing, incinerating. Food can be cooked to virtual death."

What could be simpler than eating raw food? Well, in fact, there is something simpler: Eating nothing at all. "Our theory," Nearing wrote of herself and her husband, Scott, "is: the less food the better in life, as long as you get enough." Flying against all conventional wisdom, the Nearings skipped breakfast, subsisting until noon on herb tea. Think your mother would sign on to this idea? Well, I repeat that Scott Nearing died at age one hundred and Helen at ninety. Both did hard, manual labor till near the end. Helen, ironically, drove into a tree near her home. She was the driver and sole occupant of the car.

Agree with the Nearings or not, among the most important things we can learn from them is that developing a conscious, health-minded food philosophy that works for you is—to betray my late-sixties coming of age—where it's at. Helen Nearing rightly observed that "most people eat for breakfast what the neighbors eat." Though she didn't say it explicitly, I think she was telling us that imitation—letting other people do your thinking for you about food—is not good. With food, as with other life choices, be who you are and stick to your guns.

That simplifies a lot of things. Knowing who she was, Helen had no compunction about telling her readers that "if a recipe cannot be written on the face of a 3-by-5 card, off with its head. The theme of my book will be: live hard not soft; eat hard not soft; seek fiber in foods and in life."

As you might have guessed by now, the Nearings were big on salads, starting every evening meal with a large bowl of raw greens they considered "the most important part of our diet." They plucked salad materials from "the meadow" as well as from their garden. They particularly enjoyed dandelions in season. They also ate plenty of seeds—no shocker there. And, I'm pleased to report, they were frugivorous—fruit-eating—folks.

Helen, who had already won my heart with her cantankerous charm, won my eternal gratitude with this revelation: "The prize fruit of all, in our estimation, of which we never tire, is the apple. It does not cloy the taste. It is neither too sweet nor too sour. No matter how many you eat you can never get sick on them or of them."

Being a grower and peddler of apples, what better advertisement for my wares could I find than that?

Living the Good Life, a bible—along with *Walden*—for simple-living advocates, was first published in 1954. The Nearings summarized their philosophy of food this way: "Good food should be grown on whole soil, be eaten whole, unprocessed, and garden fresh. Even the best products of the best soils lose more or less of their nutritive value if they are processed. Any modification at all is likely to reduce the nutritive value of a whole food."

Puts most of us to shame, doesn't it? Though we might not agree that no other approach to "good" food exists, the Nearings challenged and stretched us all. They compelled us to reflect on our philosophy of food, on the choices we make every day, and on food's primal rootedness in life itself. They were big-picture thinkers for whom nothing was too small to make a difference. Read them and we have no choice but to ask, "What is *my* connection with the earth? How am *I* living my life? What will *I* do to make a difference?"

CHAPTER 8
Soul Work

"*Let your soul turn always, not to desire the more, but the less.*"

—Saint John of the Cross

"*As we live and as we are, Simplicity—with a capital S—is difficult to comprehend nowadays. We are no longer truly simple. We no longer live in simple terms or places. Life is a more complex struggle now. It is now valiant to be simple: a courageous thing to even want to be simple. It is a spiritual thing to comprehend what simplicity means.*"

—Frank Lloyd Wright

According to most men I know, our mothers are or were saints, women who set the standard for perfection—and all the rest of the world pales by comparison! Even Richard Nixon, never noted for keeping company with saints, allowed that his mother might have been one. With some trepidation, then, I offer you a quote from my sainted mother, Miriam Lindsey Levering—a Quaker, like Nixon's mother. Ironically, it's a quote about perfection.

"Moses," my mother once remarked, "had his body in the water before the Red Sea parted. You take the self that you have, and you put it in the water."

That "self that you have," my mother was saying, is anything but perfect. And if you wait for self-perfection before you "advance on faith"—a favorite expression of Miriam Levering's—you'll never accomplish a thing. Faith, my mother believed, could move mountains—or part the Red Sea. But what you have faith in is not the hope of an ideal self, but the ability of flawed mortals to achieve wondrous things.

Catholic theologian Henry Nouwen makes much the same point: "You don't think your way into a new kind of living. You live your way into a new kind of thinking."

In other words, you act, you try something, you're not on the sidelines armchair-quarterbacking, a pot-shotting critic-at-large. You're in the game.

The wisdom of Miriam Levering—a peace and international-law advocate who played a vital nongovernmental role in the development of the United Nations-sponsored Law of the Sea Treaty—is worth remembering when we face our own implacable Red Sea. As is Nouwen's insight that courageous living can lead to inspired thinking. When it comes to what I call soul work—the effort to align ourselves with something larger than ourselves, the effort to mature spiritually—it's important to recognize that it's never too soon to start. No matter how unworthy you may feel, no matter how unsure of your ability you are, that "self that you have" is good to go.

Still, we hesitate. Surely, others—people who seem to walk the talk of spiritual alignment—are better at this than we are. Yearning to evolve spiritually, we're tempted to attach ourselves to gurus. And gurus abound in the soul-work business. The American spiritual guru menu offers quite a gustatory selection, from sun-dried New Agers on one end of the spectrum to deep-fried fundamentalists in virtually all religions on the other. And if one guru is not enough, we can always order à la carte—a guru here, a guru there, adding up, we hope, to a satisfying spiritual feast.

Forgotten in our follow-the-guru culture—a curious phenomenon, given our lip service to the virtues of doing our own thinking—is the stark fact that, spiritually, in the end, we must look deeply into ourselves, facing our inner Red Sea with whatever strength may come to us from God or whatever forces we invoke to help us. All but forgotten, too, is the organic connection between spirituality and simplicity. Too many of our contemporary gurus want it all. They offer us the heady fragrance of transcendence, yes—but on closer inspection, they offer it with all the trappings of material "success."

Thoreau, at his famous pond, knew better. The quintessential transcendentalist, a man who in his meticulous scrutiny of nature inferred transcendental divinity in our mundane world, Thoreau understood that soul work eschews what money can buy. "Superfluous wealth," he insisted, "can buy superfluities only. Money is not required to buy one necessary of the soul."

Simplicity and Spirituality

A few miles down the modern highway from Walden Pond, I used up much of my quota of salad days at Harvard Divinity School, where Thoreau's compatriot Ralph Waldo Emerson delivered his famous "transcendental eyeball" lecture, startling the proper Boston intelligentsia with an image of the divine never dreamt of—as Hamlet would say—in their philosophy.

Controversy has not been a stranger at Harvard Divinity. In my era, as now, the school has rocked the boat of conventional Christianity by emphasizing the spiritual legitimacy of other religions, particularly at the school's Center for the Study of World Religions, a physically unimposing, yet intellectually formidable, enclave of scholars from many faith traditions.

It is, to be sure, world-class scholars who rock that Christian boat. Their recognition that religious diversity is a fact of life on a multicultural, ever-evolving planet has made more than a few old-line passengers a tad green at the gills.

Religious diversity is not an offshore phenomenon alone. The United States has become—since the passage of the 1965 Immigration Act—the most religiously diverse nation on earth. In the best of all worlds, religious diversity—which implies the existence of many faiths but not necessarily engagement and understanding among them—leads to pluralism. Religious pluralism, writes Harvard professor Diana L. Eck in her book *Encountering God*, means that truth "is not the exclusive or inclusive possession of any one tradition or community. Therefore the diversity of communities, traditions, understandings of the truth, and visions of God is not an obstacle for us to overcome, but an opportunity for our energetic engagement and dialogue with one another. It does not mean giving up our commitments; rather, it means opening up those commitments to the give-and-take of mutual discovery, understanding, and, indeed, transformation."

My own exposure at Harvard Divinity to the richness of world religions led me to one overriding conclusion: Simplicity lies at the core of spirituality. Certainly, most of the faith traditions have embraced simplicity in one form or another, acknowledging the lapidary wisdom of Jesus when he says that if your eye is sound, your whole body will be full of light. Simplicity, in this spiritual sense, is a way of cleaning the lens of sight, of clearing away all that obscures

Across Cultural Simplicity

Across many cultures, simplicity has long been regarded as a way of helping humans address what Protestant theologian Paul Tillich calls the "ultimate concerns" of existence. Wealth is transitory, the Koran stresses, and the pursuit of wealth can lead to spiritual death. "Unless a man is simple," goes an old Bengali song, "he cannot recognize God, the Simple One."

the larger truths beyond ourselves. Inner simplicity, we might name this response to the challenge of the infinite—a simplicity that cherishes, above all things, the inner life of the spirit.

One of the primary truths of the life of the spirit is the idea of divine "enoughness." "The rich man," the Talmud reminds us, "is the man who is satisfied with what he has." "He who knows he has enough is rich" is the wisdom of the *Tao Te Ching*. True wealth, says Jesus memorably in Luke, is being "rich toward God." Time and again, with a dazzling array of metaphors, Jesus teaches us that our real treasures are God's spiritual gifts, eternal and nonmaterial, available to anyone willing to receive them.

In his book *The Joy of Living and Dying in Peace*, the Dalai Lama affirms what is essentially the same revelation from his embattled Tibetan Buddhist tradition. "In life," he writes, "you face hardship to amass food and wealth, but at death you have to leave it. Who knows how your wealth will be used by those who inherit it? For a few days they may grieve for you, but soon they will be squabbling over their share. This is how your life is spent."

Jesus might have put the matter more metaphorically, but here lies the fundamental insight of simplicity, cutting across disparate spiritual traditions. Use your time here wisely, the Dalai Lama is telling us. Life is short and of infinite value, and there is much to distract and tempt us away from what is eternal in our nature. Determine what you *really* need. Finding your real treasures and understanding their full value—that's where simplicity and spirituality converge. The rest is transitory. The rest, ultimately, will have no meaning.

Becoming a Spiritual Traveler

Every Tuesday evening, I make the winding, pastoral drive down the Blue Ridge Parkway to Meadows of Dan, Virginia, on the rolling Blue Ridge plateau, where, in a modest country living room overlooking a tranquil pond, a group of a dozen or so gathers in the name of what we hope is spiritual growth.

Hosted by Felecia Shelor, a businesswoman, ordained minister, and Mideast peace activist whose Appalachian heritage is Primitive Baptist, it's an eclectic group: a handful of Pentecostal Christians with varying interpretations of the New Testament; a Quaker minister originally from the Czech Republic; several self-described "spiritualists"; a retired MIT physicist with Catholic roots who attends an Episcopal church; a lapsed Catholic entrepreneur attracted to Zen; and even an agnostic or two.

Having no agenda other than the voluntary invitation to pray, we're likely to talk about anything from Paul's notions of Christian love to the urgent need for building bridges with Muslims. Yet underlying any conversation is the assumption that all of us in the group—as individuals and in some unspoken sense collectively—are on a spiritual journey.

The metaphor of a journey, so widely invoked these days, is a way of visualizing what it means to grow spiritually. Journeys, after all, thread their way through the great religious narratives. Sacred texts from around the world are replete with travels that often suggest startling correspondences between inner and outer journeys.

But beyond that, whether it's a journey to the Himalayas or to the edge of your backyard, the idea is not only to reach a destination but also to be transformed in some way. In fact, some would argue, like the philosopher Gabriel Marcel, that the journey itself—the ongoing transitions we experience as we live our lives—is the real work of the soul. Our condition, Marcel writes, "is that of a traveler. . . . It is precisely the soul that is the traveler; it is of the soul and the soul alone that we can say with supreme truth that 'being' necessarily means 'being on the way.' "

Spiritually, then, perhaps we are all "on the way," ticketed for a destination unknown to some and known (or so they insist) to others. But in the going, we will inevitably change. If and when we reach a final destination, who is that person who has reached it? Surely, despite our genetic coding, it is not the same person who embarked on the journey, whose spiritual growth, continuously adapting to the unpredictability of inner travel, carried him or her to an unanticipated place.

If "life is a journey, and the journey itself home," as the Japanese poet Basho contends, then where we live spiritually is an ever-changing domain. In that sense, our spiritual odyssey resembles physicists' modern understanding of the cosmos—the "unexpected universe," in the phrase of author Loren Eisley. It's a world, in the words of physicist David Oliver, that is "unpredictably, unknowingly wild beyond scientific law," where matter is perpetually in flux and new realities are created by the nanosecond. It's a world, Oliver observes, "in which mystery is deepened and continually born anew." It's a world, arguably, in which both thought and action help to invent reality, in which the dancer cannot be separated from the dance.

In Alice's Wonderland, conventional, sensory-based conceptions of the solidity of what is real—of a mechanical system made of separate objects—melt like April snow. Indeed, what is real in this vertiginous picture of our cosmic home is, perhaps, subject to the relation between particles or constellations of matter, between the observer and the observed. We live not in Creation—a made "thing"—but in eternal becoming, a "magnificent frolic," as author Barry Wood calls it, a dynamic, eternal dance of energy.

What we carry with us, then—what allows for the continuity of growth in a finite life span—is an ever-widening ability to follow the binary stars of mystery and change. "All is change," says the Greek philosopher Heraclitus. "Only change is changeless."

And yet we are eternal, tracing our ancestry, chemically and spiritually, some 14 billion years to the unthinkable origins of the universe. This is our life wrapped in human skin, following mystery and change, their holiness and beauty. Together, they are the one constant—the North Star for the spiritual traveler.

Inner simplicity, then, is clear-sightedness, the evolving ability to steer by divine mystery and change across the inner and outer landscapes of our journey. We do need tools for it, tools that come not only from the wisdom traditions but also from science, philosophy, and the arts; from persons, places, and occurrences, often unexpected; and from the diversity of life itself, from our biosphere.

Yet in another sense, we don't. We already possess those tools. They exist within us, waiting only to be used.

Finding Quiet Time

Recently in our gathering at Felecia Shelor's home in Meadows of Dan, a guest appeared, a woman in her early forties who is a friend of a woman in the group. During the course of a winter evening, we learned that our guest craves a simpler life. In a city in North Carolina, she has, as she put it, "what the Joneses have"—a very large house, an SUV, and all the other material trappings.

"But it doesn't make me happy," she told us. And with children, a job, a husband, and a large house to attend to, she has almost no time for herself. *Almost.* "I do," she said, "have five minutes a day of quiet time. Time that I've set aside for myself."

Time is the raw material of inner simplicity. Without it, the things we need to do to mature spiritually have little chance to develop. Our guest's frustration with her lack of personal time was almost palpable.

Yet something gave me hope about new possibilities opening up in this woman's life. She had, after all, found two and a half hours to drive to our meeting place and take part in our conversation. And remembering Miriam Levering's injunction to "take the self that you have" and "put it in the water," it occurred to me that those five minutes were, indeed, putting her in the water. To invoke my mother's metaphor, the Red Sea hadn't parted yet, but the woman was in the water. In those five minutes, she told us, she prays.

She reaches out beyond herself and asks God for help in finding a better way to live.

Lack of time was once *the* issue for Cathy Whitmire, author of *Plain Living*, an anthology of Quaker writings. Quakers often use the term *plain living* rather than *simplicity*. On a chilly December day, Wanda, Cathy, and I were toasty as could be sitting on our plain wooden benches inside the Friends (Quaker) Meeting in Cambridge, Massachusetts, where Wanda and I often attended the "meetings for worship," as Quakers call their worship service, when we were students at Harvard. A shaft of afternoon sunlight receded stealthily down Cathy's bench toward the window that filtered it, and Cathy moved with the sunlight, basking in its rays. Often smiling, her serene face told a different story from the one she had lived through.

Twenty-five years ago, Cathy said, she was an overworked health-care administrator trying desperately to simplify her life. At the end of each calendar year, she'd try to think of new ways to create more nonwork time. She found herself continuing to truncate her sleep time and taking the latest time-management seminar, as if less sleep and better time management would fix her problem. But she remained as time pressured, as work overloaded, as ever. Nothing external was offering her a simpler life.

The Ears of Your Heart

Then, Cathy told us, a friend suggested she look not outward but inward to simplify her life. By looking within, her friend believed, Cathy would discover her innermost priorities. And once she accomplished that, she would know what she had to do.

Cathy followed her friend's advice.

What she told us at the Cambridge Friends Meeting would, I suspect, be her own advice to the woman who visited our group. "The most important place to start," she said, "is with inner attentiveness—learning to listen within. This is not always easy to do. I found that when I was first starting out, everything from the vet's appointment with the dog to whether or not I turned off the stove with the teakettle would sift through my head. And that learning to quiet my inner noise was the first step.

"There are several things I learned to do. I'd read something spiritual before I tried to listen within with the ears of my heart. Sometimes, I'd do a breathing exercise, where as I breathed in deeply, I would imagine breathing in peace, and as I exhaled, I imagined exhaling fear."

Gradually, enhanced by the once-a-week, communal, inner-attentiveness experience of Quaker silent meeting, Cathy discovered the innermost priorities that led her to leave her job. A series of yard sales left her spiritually buoyant, unencumbered by "stuff." Ultimately, she enrolled at Harvard Divinity School, then moved to Maine after graduation. There, she found satisfying work with reasonable hours and continued to pare away any activity or possession that was not, in her words, "essential."

What is essential, Cathy gently insists, can be known by anyone who steadfastly looks inward. She agrees with Plotinus when he insists that "to the possession of the self, the way is inward." Quaker language for what this inner experience, this self-possession, is varies widely. Some call it the experience of the "inner light," of "God within us." Whatever the figurative language, Cathy, like many Quakers, attests to the transforming power of an inner encounter with divine mystery. Simplicity, in her life, flows from a spiritual source.

"Plain living," Cathy writes in her book, "is a form of inward simplicity that leads us to the 'still, small voice' of God's claim upon our lives. It is both a spiritual lens and a discipline of holy obedience. This way of living simplifies our lives because when we focus our energies on what we discern by listening within, we are able to release the extraneous activities and possessions that clutter our path."

I think that any of us, no matter how unhinged by the pace of contemporary life, can learn both from Cathy and from the urban visitor to our group's weekly gathering. To make room for quiet time—to turn off the TV set, or the radio when driving our car; to walk into "a room of one's own," in Virginia Woolf's phrase, and close the door—is to give ourselves a chance to listen to what astronomers call "deep space." We become, to extend that metaphor, spiritual radio astronomers, our inner radio telescopes attuned to signals from the source of our being.

Crossing the Bridge of Prayer

To distinguish "inner attentiveness" from what many people would simply call "prayer" may be too fine a distinction. Is "learning to listen within" the same sort of engagement with the source of our being as what many folks think of as prayer? What is prayer, exactly? And how can we weave it into the fabric of inner simplicity?

What we in the West call prayer spans our globe in a multiplicity of forms, bridging Hinduism and Islam—and certain strands of Buddhism—with the Judeo-Christian and Native American traditions in which many Americans have been steeped. Prayer, writes Sophy Burnham in *The Path of Prayer*, "is quite simply a yearning of the heart." Elsewhere, she defines it as "the doorway to the thin places between the physical and spiritual worlds, the shadowy portal through which we see into the other dimensions and through which we draw down spiritual help."

Saint Augustine defines prayer as, simply, love. "True, whole prayer," he tells us, "is nothing but love."

His fellow Christian Felecia Shelor, host of our Tuesday-evening gatherings, thinks of prayer as "surrender." It is, she says, a way of acknowledging our dependence on God. In surrendering our ego to a higher power, Felecia says, we practice the humility that is for her at the heart of Christianity. Praying to God, who both loves and forgives us, we surrender our claims of self to the will of God revealed for Christians most profoundly in the New Testament.

David Oliver, the former MIT physicist who is also a member of our group, relates that his own ability to pray took root when he read a number of the spiritual commentaries of the Desert Fathers (and Mothers), who lived in the Egyptian desert during the fourth and fifth centuries. The flight of Anthony, Agathon, Theodora, Sarah, and others occurred, writes theologian Henry Nouwen, as a "way to escape the tempting conformity of the world." According to Nouwen in *The Way of the Heart*, "the words *flee, be silent* and *pray* summarize the spirituality of the desert. They indicate the three ways of preventing the world from shaping us in its image and are thus the three ways to the life in the Spirit."

For David Oliver, doors have opened to prayer through the solitude and silence he experiences—much like the men and women who inspired him, though in a different time and landscape—on his Blue Ridge Mountain farm. There—without a television set, answering machine, or cell phone—David communes unimpeded with God, who has endowed the universe described by modern physics with the ultimate freedom: the freedom to love.

In the end, each person prays in a way that may be hard to translate for others. Often, the impulse for prayer and the prayer itself are inarticulate within the heart. Yet "it is better," as Gandhi tells us, "in prayer to have a heart without words than words without a heart."

For me, the ubiquitous belief that prayer can "draw down spiritual help" converges with the idea of inner attentiveness. In listening to an inner voice, we "attend"—in the words of Protestant theologian Richard Neibuhr—to the implied ability of that voice to propel us toward truth and to help us. For all the other human emotions that may infuse it—gratitude, hope, love, and fear, to name a few—prayer is never far from the implication that we are inviting empowerment from a divine source.

Opening ourselves to prayer can be difficult. We are, in the end, alone with whatever it is that continuously unfurls our cosmos and that—physically, at least—will demolish us and erase our human form. The survivor in us— Darwin's child, the warrior—can raise an angry and frightened fist.

"Deep within every man," writes philosopher Soren Kierkegaard, "there lies the dread of being alone in the world, forgotten by God, overlooked among the tremendous household of millions and millions." In the face of Kierkegaard's existential dread, prayer can seem a cruel joke, a futile, fearful cry beamed absurdly into the void.

There is prayer like that; I, for one, have experienced it. And there are moments—my mother's death was one—in which prayer seems to offer no solace. For my part, though, I draw inspiration from the woman who visited our group. "Prayer," she told us, had been "very awkward at first." Like many who struggle with the thought of prayer, prayers she'd deemed insincere or egotistical had turned her off in the past.

Yet on the path toward inner simplicity, prayer is one universally potent way to express our soul's longing to forge its deepest connections. It can help clean the lens of sight, giving us a chance to experience divine mystery from the deep well of our yearning and sincerity. Ultimately, perhaps the one metaphor I'd choose in describing prayer is the familiar one of a bridge—a bridge to the spiritual depths of other people, life forms, and cultures, a bridge to the eternal in our nature.

Shamelessly politicized, made ludicrous by literalism, and often merely an instrument for authoritarian views and prescriptions, prayer has been much abused in our era. We have witnessed quite a field day for skeptics.

But prayer offered out of real, existential aloneness—the inescapable human experience of collective and individual anguish—remains our most poignant form of utterance. Without prayer, we are the most desiccated corner of that desert in which the Desert Fathers and Mothers lived. With prayer, or even the hope that prayer will come, our desiccation draws water. Our corner is barren no more, a place where life can even flourish.

Trying Meditation

Like prayer, the practice of meditation spans East and West and assumes a virtually infinite number of forms. With the increasing popularity of Buddhist teachings and practices in the West, as well as the continuing interest in Hindu-based or -inspired wisdom, it would take a few lifetimes to sample all the meditation practices available through various teachers, institutes, and retreat centers. Much of what is being offered sounds daunting to the novice—day-long, backbreaking "sitting" sessions that promise consciousness breakthroughs of various sorts; reams of esoteric concepts from various strains of Buddhism and Hinduism that can make a thunderous thud as they fall on Western ears.

For years in college and graduate school, I studied Buddhism and, to a lesser extent, Hinduism, drawn to these two traditions so ostensibly alien to my own Quaker Christian upbringing, yet put off by the dense thickets of conceptual language and by the apparent rigor of meditative practice toward the goal of release from the grip of attachment. My older sister Miriam— "Merry," our family calls her—was named for my mother. From her perch as a scholar of Buddhism and occasional practitioner of various meditations, she encouraged me to go deeper.

It was to no avail. Life was difficult enough. Who needed to add one more arduous pursuit?

In 1998, though, when I was well into my forties, an arduous pursuit of a different sort led to a modest breakthrough. After harvesting and selling an unusually small apple crop that autumn at our orchard, I had a chance to realize the lifelong ambition of trekking to the base of Mount Everest in northeastern Nepal, at nearly nineteen thousand feet in elevation.

Lugging a forty-pound backpack and enduring long, frigid nights in a sleeping bag, I spent nearly four weeks in November and December in the domain of the native Sherpas, walking some two hundred miles with my guide and translator, Dok Dahal, and frequently talking with native folks who were practitioners of Tibetan Buddhism, including a number of the Sherpa monks who populate the cliff-hugging monasteries beneath the stupendous Himalayan peaks. It was a firsthand encounter with Buddhist culture in the Khumbu region along the Tibetan border, where prayer flags flutter in the icy wind and copper prayer wheels spin, glinting in the sun, at the touch of a hand. Along the trek, sitting on a boulder or at the edge of a frosty bunk bed, I began, for the first time in my life, to meditate.

The Sherpas themselves were a primary inspiration, as was the journey itself, a midlife passage of sorts that begged for coming to grips with mutinous inner demons. But I also carried in my backpack an incisive little book I'd picked up in Kathmandu. Titled simply *How to Meditate*, it was written by Kathleen McDonald, a Tibetan Buddhist nun. The book offered lucid, unintimidating instruction on ways to start—and later expand—meditation.

What I learned was that, in its most basic, "stabilizing meditation" form, anyone—and I mean *anyone*—can meditate. You don't have to be esoteric about it. You certainly don't need to be a Buddhist, though many would argue that this would enhance the experience. All you have to do is sit comfortably but alertly and observe your breath.

Why observe your breath? Or why visualize an image or concept, other forms of what McDonald calls "single-pointed concentration"? Remarkably, there are Buddha-knows-how-many books and teachers that address this subject. One can assess the rewards of meditation all the way to nirvana and back, adding layer after layer of meaning and nuance. These days particularly, much is made of meditation as a way of helping us to live in the present moment. The ramifications of breath observation and its kindred are almost infinite.

But what I've discovered thus far is in one sense simple. Kathleen McDonald is accurate when she writes that observing your breath "brings an immediate sense of spaciousness and allows us to see the workings of our mind more clearly, both during the meditation and throughout the rest of the day."

The basic reward here could hardly be more delicious. By focusing on a single point—in this case, your breath—you quell the helter-skelter mind storms that, particularly in our hyperstimulative culture, threaten at times to engulf us. "The inner noise," Cathy Whitmire calls it, the maddening din of racing thoughts.

In this form of meditation, you don't try to erase those thoughts. You let them come and go, always returning to the rhythm of observing your breath. By practicing regular, uninterrupted meditation of this elemental sort in twenty- or thirty-minute sessions, you begin to let go of those thoughts that once seemed so oppressive. The mind grows calmer—more "spacious," as McDonald suggests—letting thoughts and sensations simply "be," knowing they will pass.

Before long, you begin to understand how easy it is to become thought driven—obsessed with something or someone that, from a more "spacious" perspective, has no business laying claim to so much of your consciousness. As McDonald suggests, you see your own mind more clearly and have the freedom to act accordingly. It becomes much easier to let go, to be less attached. In my own experience, things get better in troubled relationships, including my own sometimes troubled relationship with myself. And things get better with whatever name we give the source of our spiritual life.

The practice of yoga, I'm told, can accomplish much the same thing. An old friend of mine from high school, Bill Beamer, teaches karate classes. He knows what I mean within the context of his highly focused experience of karate. Others sing the praises of "analytical meditation"—meditating on anger, for example, in such a focused way that, over a number of sessions, the meditator "becomes" anger and in some way comprehends its emptiness and is transformed. This I can't tell you about. What I do know is that, for me and for many others, the simplest form of meditation can make the mind more "spacious."

"Walking Meditation"

Though my version employs a straight-backed chair or sometimes a tree trunk, meditation need not be limited to a body at rest. Meditation on the move is possible—in household chores, for example, or in what Zen monk and author Thich Nhat Hanh calls "walking meditation," in which the walker moves at a slower-than-normal pace, without any particular destination, synchronizing breath with steps, stopping occasionally to be "truly present" with a stone or a tree, practicing "deep attention."

What is meditation, ultimately? Is there a sense in which it is also prayer, or what Cathy Whitmire calls "inner attentiveness," or what Quaker author Daniel A. Seeger calls "inner silence . . . a gentle practice of letting stray thoughts fall away as we notice them, and returning our attention to the present"?

I don't have answers. For me, it may be that my long walk in a vivid Buddhist corner of Nepal—and the beginning of meditation—returned me, full circle, to Quaker roots that are perhaps not as alien to Buddhism as I once thought. Journeys, it's been said, often allow us to know our home for the first time.

However that may be, consider meditation as you go about your necessary soul work. Meditation need not dislodge prayer or any of the other bridges to the immensity of being. It may in fact be, as it was for me, the very next thing you need.

Looking for Love

We're all experts on love. Aside—a cynic might say—from money and sex, it's the subject that engages us most. Love has been written and sung about and dramatized in films, plays, and television shows so many times that what's left to say about it? Paul, in the New Testament, portrays love as the greatest gift from God, and many a preacher and Sunday-school teacher has equated love *with* God. What more do we need to know? Besides, we've all experienced love, haven't we? What's new under the sun about love?

Nothing, of course. But it's a good thing to remind ourselves that, as life hurtles by, saving time and space to love and be loved is perhaps our greatest gift to ourselves. "To cheat oneself out of love," writes Kierkegaard in his classic *Works of Love*, "is the most terrible deception; it is an eternal loss for which there is no reparation, either in time or in eternity."

Simplicity and love are intimate companions. Since money can't buy it, love in its essential form—beyond what's fair or "right"; beyond generosity or pride; beyond, arguably, even hope—comes only when we give it a chance to blossom. The practice of simplicity frees us to give love an honest chance. Simplicity strips away love of possessions, love of money, and excessive self-love. In their place is a full view of the person in front of you, the person with whom you share a life, or—as in Thornton Wilder's timeless play, *Our Town*—the persons with whom you share your small corner of the world.

A simpler life clears the stage for the "Full Monty"—not the gamely nude Brits of the popular film, but the uniqueness of your life's cast of characters. Simplicity, in a word, gets personal. It finds the person, perhaps in a dark corner, and helps us see what light is there—the potential for growth, one soul's infinite complexity, real wealth.

Love is not words but actions. Professions of love without the currency of time and effort ring hollow. Love undermined by envy is the power of love negated. A simpler life in which we find pleasure, even joy, in timeless things gives envy, love's assassin, small chance to take aim.

Still, no one said love is easy. The difficulty of proactive love in the play of emotions will forever challenge us. The smallest gestures and the simplest kindnesses will always make a difference. Simplicity, which gives us time to breathe, gives us also some measure of the strength we need to love.

In looking for love, we need look no farther than ourselves. We choose to love or not love, to be loved or not be loved, contingent on the inner demons that beset human nature, demons that will destroy love or that we will conquer.

Love, in the final analysis, is ours to make real. Just as we choose a simpler life from a tantalizing menu of American dreams, we choose love in the way that we live and in the effort to make love work. Look for it, find it, do it—that's the way a good love song should go. Love and a simpler life can make beautiful music together.

Shedding

In her book *Gift from the Sea*, first published in 1955, Anne Morrow Lindbergh writes of a time spent alone at her house near the ocean, a time getting back to basics, as we might say in our era, a time for simplicity in both its outer and inner forms. Of life at the beach, she writes, "One learns first of all . . . the art of shedding: how little one can get along with, not how much."

For Lindbergh, a small suitcase filled with clothes, a "bare sea-shell of a cottage," a few sticks of furniture, and a space she didn't worry about cleaning fastidiously were heaven itself. "What a relief it is!" she exclaims, contrasting the simplicity of beach living with her life and obligations in the city. "I am shedding pride," she writes. In the shedding of inner as well as outer burdens, she hopes "to learn something I can carry back into my worldly life."

What Lindbergh learned—what all of us can learn—is the art of letting go. Materially, many of us, like Cathy Whitmire, have experienced the "high" of getting rid of "stuff," that purging experience in which, in some hard-to-define sense, we are reborn, at least for a time.

But Lindbergh's letting-go lesson went beyond material things. "I shall ask into my shell only those friends," she writes, "with whom I can be completely honest. I find I am shedding hypocrisy in human relationships. What a rest that will be! The most exhausting thing in life, I have discovered, is being insincere. That is why so much of social life is exhausting; one is wearing a mask. I have shed my mask."

Shedding your mask—what a mind-boggling idea! Imagine your life utterly devoid of pretense in human relationships. What would it be like to be free to be yourself, to live just as you really are without trying to impress, please, nudge, sell, or in any other way wear a mask, to never endure the exhaustion of insincerity?

Though difficult to achieve, it's certainly worth imagining. And in doing our soul work, Lindbergh's implicit invitation to join her in that new life has profound relevance. For as the soul "knows itself"—as we mature spiritually—we face the ever-more-urgent question of how we present our real selves to others. In our culture, not everyone will endorse our simpler life. Not everyone will want to enter or spend time in our "bare sea-shell of a cottage." We will inevitably be seen by some as unfit to conduct a life in the real world.

And in a culture where intolerance vies daily with tolerance for the upper hand, we may be seen by some as spiritually unworthy as well. True religion, some folks tell us, has little to do with inner simplicity; it's all about whose side God is on. And from true religion, some folks say, flows material prosperity.

Thus, learning to let go is a necessity for the spiritual traveler into inner simplicity. In revealing one's true self and values, we let go of old inclinations and of relationships—or the foundations of relationships—that once seemed obligatory. We shed our old skins.

This doesn't mean that we let go of proven sources of strength. Richard Gregg, the Quaker author and activist who first elaborated the concept of what he calls "voluntary simplicity," tells a story about his encounter with Mahatma Gandhi. "We were talking," Gregg writes, "about simple living, and I said that it was easy for me to give up most things but that I had a greedy mind and wanted to keep my many books."

"He said, 'Then don't give them up. As long as you derive inner help and comfort from anything, you should keep it. If you were to give it up in a mood of self-sacrifice or out of a stern sense of duty, you would continue to want it back, and that unsatisfied want would make trouble for you. Only give up a thing when you want some other condition so much that the thing no longer has any attraction for you, or when it seems to interfere with that which is more greatly desired.' "

Letting go—shedding—when the time is right is Gandhi's wisdom, and the wisdom of the ages. The distillation we all know by heart—that he who loses himself gains himself—transcends cultures and faith traditions. Its wisdom applies to every impulse in our bones to make life simpler.

Spiritually speaking, too, less is more. "Not to desire the more," as Saint John of the Cross tells us, "but the less"—that's the bottom line.

Journal Writing

Practical, day-to-day tools for inner simplicity vary with the practitioner. Love music? Music, then, can become a tool. Love people? Involvement in the life of your community may be the best tool in your "soul workshop."

Active reflection, though, is what the soul needs to keep in shape. It's the equivalent of the early-morning jog, the after-work workout in the gym. It's hard to think of a simpler, more muscular mode of reflection than writing in a journal. True, the virgin pages of a journal are also a great place to vent, to write ten searing pages on the boss's latest outrage. But venting, as a form of soul work, is not all bad. Often, it's the warmup before more meaningful reflection, the adrenaline-steeped calisthenics, the thunder before the soaking rain.

Journal writing has few rules. It is, in fact, one of the few ways in which an adult is truly free to play. Your mind is free. It can go anywhere it wishes, shuttle back and forth in time, choose any subject. Like the still surface of a pond, the pages form a mirror. Your mind and soul lie bare before you, uncensored, increasingly un-self-conscious as you go forward in one sitting, as you practice "journaling" over a period of months or years. Reading old pages of a journal, you can see the footprints of your journey, trace your progress, remember a former incarnation, marvel at the changes, and look ahead to the soul work yet to come.

Journal writing need not be scheduled, though having a regular time and place is the right idea if you thrive on regularity. But once it becomes a useful tool, it's good not to let the writing lapse for long.

To get started, find a quiet spot and let the ink flow as it will. Don't try to force the writing; just let it come to you, the mind spilling naturally onto the page. This isn't a term paper or a corporate report. It's not for anyone's eyes but your own.

As you write, think of the space that surrounds you as, in some sense, sacred space. You need not be solemn in this notion. The point of Virginia Woolf's "room of one's own" is that your life, too, matters. The "force" is with you—hence, you write in a sacred space. Journal writing is play, but it's serious play. What bodies forth is a serious self, a person to be reckoned with. But the birthing is best if it remains playful, open to anything that comes.

Let the scribbling begin.

Soul Gardening

Nature calls us. We listen or we don't listen, depending on our life circumstances, on whether we have the time and space to answer the call, on whether we're in the mood. But the call never ceases. The flower children had it right. We are nature's children—naked in the Garden, that is. As we now know, that implies not only sweetness and light but also a Darwinian free-for-all, where life survives only when it can.

Estranged from nature, our souls implode. Anyone who has ever observed children from relentlessly urban environments coming alive to the natural world knows intuitively the whole story about human origins and the thirst we have for connection with what formed us. To try to reestablish that connection, many of us take to the water in boats, to hiking trails, to ski slopes, to the golf course. Even the sad parade of riding mowers across ornately manicured lawns testifies to the human yearning to return to the Garden. We crave our natural connections, sanitized or not.

Ellen Hoffs, our longtime friend from our Los Angeles days, found her own way back to the Garden four years ago. To do that, Ellen, now in her sixties, journeyed no farther than her front and back yards, patches of prime Santa Monica real estate. Her backyard was a combination of concrete (primarily for a paddleball court) and lawn grass.

After many arduous years as a freelance journalist battling fire-breathing editors and health problems, Ellen craved a gentler life and a new challenge that would return her, in some sense, to the postage-stamp victory gardens she had known as a child immigrant in Los Angeles. The daughter of German Jews, she was fortunate to have a new lease on life in coastal Southern California's Mediterranean climate.

And so—utterly in character, and with the help of her husband, psychiatrist and poet Malcolm Hoffs—Ellen did the unconventional. Out went the backyard asphalt and grass, creating for a time piles of unsightly rubble. In—over the course of several years, and after she returned to school to study horticulture—went a premeditated brew of mostly native Southern California plants, particularly grasses and sedges, along with iron and ceramic sculptures and reclaimed "art objects" such as a rusty, old industrial conveyor belt that now forms a winding pathway through the garden. There is also a front, streetside garden consisting primarily of native plants and lawn grass.

Blending eco-friendly plants that require little water with oddments of used materials finding a new identity—old courtyard bricks that have become gate pillars, concrete slabs that now form garden paths and walls, etc.—Ellen created what she calls an "art garden," a singular environment that lures birds and feeds the soul.

On a recent visit, Ellen's garden fed our souls. Off and on for the better part of three days, Wanda and I feasted on the fragrant native plants in her front garden and on what I kiddingly described to Ellen as the "organized chaos" in the more spacious back garden, a secluded twenty-by-forty-foot nook walled off from the street, where rusted sculptures, hoary benches, and the winding conveyor belt draw the eye amid waist-high grasses and sedges that toss in the breeze off the Pacific.

Along the street beyond Ellen's wall, her neighbors still "mow, blow, and go," as the local saying has it, contributing their share to the environmental price tag seen, most days, in the less-than-azure skies of Los Angeles. But not Ellen and Mal. Their lawn work consists of tending to exquisitely beautiful plants in the back garden that is, in Ellen's phrase, "a furry meadow."

One evening when Ellen was upstairs, Mal Hoffs—in the warm glow of their kitchen—told me a story about his wife.

Like Ellen, Mal is quick to laugh. A wry, puckish pleasure crinkles his face and suffuses his body, kept young, I suspect, not only by his work in Ellen's garden but by his zest for life, for all things original and adventurous. Brooklyn born and raised, a doctor's son and now a grandfather of three, Mal is the sort of friend anyone would want, never stinting on time, honesty, or affection. But what struck me at that moment—as it had many times before—was the intensity of his delight in Ellen's passions.

And why not? In her garden, she's done it again, throwing herself body and soul into something worth doing. "She's out there at ten o'clock at night," Mal told me. "I got her this little headlamp—like a miner's lamp, kind of—that she'll wear out there at night. And she'll be out there thinking about the garden, maybe a change she's going to make, something she hasn't thought of yet.

It's like the way a painter thinks about a painting, mulling it over, rethinking what it is, looking at it from a different perspective. Living with it. That's the way Ellen is with her garden."

I asked Ellen, early the next morning in rosy February light that angled over the wall into her garden, about Mal's portrayal of her. She laughed, agreeing with him, and agreeing with me when I remarked that she probably never wanted to "finish" this garden. Like nature itself, her garden is always in flux.

"You know what?" she said.

"What?"

"Even when I was a little girl, what I really wanted to be was an old woman with a garden." She laughed her lusty, life-expanding laugh that I've loved for twenty-five years. "And now, well, here I am!"

A garden, I've learned from Ellen, is a place where both plants and a soul can grow. "When I go into my garden," Ellen said, "there's something that fills me with such happiness. It's a refuge. When you're in the garden, it's only you and the garden. Nothing else makes any difference. It's the first time in my life I've felt like something is a perfect fit."

Watching our old friend at work, listening to her affectionate stories about her plants, I saw a woman connecting with something larger than herself. Ellen is taking refuge and, yes, "gentling down" as she grows older, but she's also acknowledging her niche in the immense community of organisms, her place in the life stream. As she gardens, Ellen experiences time and again the miracle of life writ both small and large—small, in the microcosm of her home in Santa Monica, her plants taking root, flowering, running the course of their life cycles; large, in the macrocosm of our biosphere and of our ultimate linkage to the cosmic sources of life.

"Even in Los Angeles!" I heard the cynic within me whisper.

Yes, even in Los Angeles.

And even where you and I are. With a demanding, fifty-seven-acre orchard for my garden, I arrived home nonetheless mulling over how I could apply Ellen's example to my Blue Ridge environment, how I could replace lawn grass with something far more creative and environmentally sound. And mulling over what that might do for my soul.

Perhaps similar thoughts will cross your mind.

Rising from the Ashes

The story of Job, a man of faith beset by every imaginable plague and horror, is in its vivid way the human story. Life is suffering. The Buddha, enshrining this idea as the first of his Four Noble Truths, takes a sharp right turn from the Judeo-Christian tradition in prescribing a course of action designed in a very practical way to eliminate suffering once and for all. About suffering, that latter tradition is of two minds: Yes, there is perhaps a way out of it, contingent on our ability to follow God's will; but no, suffering is to an equal degree inevitable in this life, just as it was for Jesus.

For me, there's an archetypal story that in a sense splits the difference between the Buddhist and Judeo-Christian notions about suffering. It's the story of the Phoenix, apparently destroyed, then rising from the ashes. It's the story of the alchemy of suffering, of creation from destruction. In that sense, it's the story of how creativity can flower within the soul.

It seems to me that creativity—the ability to imagine, and to implement that imaginative vision—flows in large part out of the wellspring of suffering. Just as nature does, we create out of what is destroyed. We pluck life from death. We emerge, tested by fire, from the ashes.

Let me tell you a story. One night in November 1996, my father's parents' house—the Red House, we called it, a two-story, frame community landmark built in 1909—caught fire and burned all night, despite heroic effort from our volunteer fire department. To this day, we don't know what caused the fire. Vacant for three years following my father's death, the house that haunted evening was filled with students on retreat from Guilford College in Greensboro, North Carolina. Fortunately, no one was hurt in the fire. But alas, in the light of dawn, only the four outer walls and my grandparents' bedroom and sitting room were intact. Inside those charred walls, the water-soaked rubble smoldered, crowned by a partially caved-in tin roof.

Within my family, at least, the demise of the Red House was a tragedy of Job-like proportions. Co-owned by my sisters and brother and Wanda and me, the Red House was our one common heirloom, a treasured repository of family history. What to do? Our insurance policy on the old house fell far short of what it would take to restore it to something like its original form. After much discussion, we decided to abandon hope for restoration. My siblings sold Wanda and me their share of the remains of the house and the surrounding three-quarter-acre tract.

For two years, Wanda and I took no action, living daily with a kind of standing corpse that loomed a hundred yards up the mountainside from our old brick farmhouse.

Then I had a thought: Why not write a play that would acknowledge the people who had built and lived in the house? We'd perform the play outdoors, in the front yard of the ruined house, a kind of "environmental theater" in which the story would unfold in its literal setting. Then, after presenting the play, we'd tear the house down, expunge the visual wound that—as long as it stared back at us from up the hill—would remind us of the anguish of the night of the fire and of our loss.

And so I wrote and presented *The Emerald Ghost*, its title taken from an Emily Dickinson poem that alludes to the color and motion of summer light immediately before thunderstorm rain falls. The play is about my father's sister, June, and my father's parents. It tells the story of June's diagnosis of schizophrenia at age eighteen, her unrequited love for a boy, and her troubled relationship with her strict Quaker parents. It is a story out of a dark closet in family history. With the presentation of the play, I hoped not only for the potential catharsis in telling a painful story, but also for closure on the Red House. If all went well, the play would allow me to move on.

What happened instead was something bordering on the miraculous. Presented over the course of three summer weekends, stunningly performed and directed, respectively, by Barbara Bates Smith and John Gulley, the play drew over twelve hundred audience members.

But that wasn't the only miracle. Primarily from towns and cities in the North Carolina Piedmont, folks were driving a long way to our mountainside, sitting out under the stars in lawn chairs, and having—if what I heard was true—the time of their lives. Live theater on our rude mountainside could be a richly meaningful experience.

A devastating fire, then, gave birth to the Cherry Orchard Theatre. Without that fire, I would never have been compelled to write the play. Without the play, we could never have caught the vision of what our mountainside offered. Still "primitive," still juxtaposing our stories with our environment, we continue to do plays in the shadow of a house that gravity and weather, in time, will bring to the earth.

And people still come. This past summer, they came by the carload to see Chekhov's masterpiece, *The Cherry Orchard*, presented on the orchard side of the ruined house, surrounded by acres of real cherry trees. At times, rain fell on the performances, but never enough for a show to be canceled. And last summer, as in all previous summers, the ruins of the house brooded over every performance, shadowing our theatrical atmosphere with the tragedy—and triumph—of real life.

From ashes, the Phoenix. In soul work, I believe, we join forces at times with something beyond ourselves at a nadir in our lives, experiencing death as we give birth to life. What wells up inside us, born of anguish and grief, is a force like the powerful current of a river, carrying us, helpless to resist, to an unknown destination.

We die, and in dying are reborn to a wider vision of our world.

Helping Creation, Helping Ourselves

There are those who maintain that the greatest soul work of all can be found simply in helping others. My mother, Miriam, taught her six children that we would never be happy unless we devoted much of our time to helping others. That lesson, multiplied to the nth degree, shapes much of the American story, most notably in recent times in the aftermath of 9/11. Few other than Scrooge himself would argue that helping others is a bad thing. But is it good for the soul? And how can a simpler life make us more helpful?

What spiritual traditions teach us is that we are accountable not only to our fellow human beings, but also to creation itself. Other people and life itself have value, and it is our responsibility to acknowledge that value and to affirm it with our actions. Money, the Koran teaches, is not a commodity, and we are obligated to share the fruits of our labor with the less fortunate. To affirm the value of other people and of our planet is to help in any way that sustains and enriches life. In helping, we link arms with creation, affirm our place within it as part of a greater whole, and help ourselves.

From the "high" we get when we help one person or many people, few would doubt that helping is good for the soul. It's a moment of enlargement, an opening into the fellowship of creation. Most of us are able to feel the kinship, the empathy, that drives our help as we give it. This is particularly true when there's a strong personal tie between the person helped and the helper.

But in helping "the planet" and people we've never seen and do not know, soul work grows more challenging. Suddenly, what and who we are helping appear to be abstractions. It's harder to connect the dots between the self that gets up in the morning and goes to work every day with something large and essentially impersonal like "the planet," or the people who live twelve thousand miles distant on that planet. The mind pulls back, continuing to live in disconnect outside the dimension of personal experience.

And yet the world outside our personal sphere desperately needs our help—not only other people on the planet, many of whom live on the edge of survival, but also other species and entire ecosystems, not to mention big-picture threats such as global warming. To live disconnected from our planet, its life forms, and the environment is to bury our heads in the sand. It's to live dangerously in the worst possible sense of that phrase.

As we do our soul work, it is more essential than ever that we challenge ourselves to help beyond the comfort zone of personal experience. The life of the planet and the well-being of our descendants depend on it.

We can offer this sort of transpersonal help in many ways.

Environmentally, we can make sound choices in our daily lives that do as little harm as possible to earth's systems, connecting the dots between our behavior and environmental health. We can support organizations working both locally and planet-wide for a better environment.

With regard to human culture, we can support the critical mission of the United Nations with our money and when we vote for our elected officials. We can support relief organizations and organizations working for social justice in a world where 2.8 billion people suffer from poverty, homelessness, and hunger. We can build cultural bridges, turning cultural "otherness" into something familiar and personal. We can travel among alien cultures, shrinking the cultural gulf not only in other countries but on what sometimes seems like the foreign soil of our own multicultural cities.

Each spiritual tradition has given us wisdom figures, teachers who summon us to the transpersonal perspective urgently needed now. If we are members of the faith community, that community can help strengthen our efforts to create positive change. As our friend the Reverend Fletcher Harper, president of the New Jersey-based Greenfaith Organization, observes, "The faith community through the civil-rights movement and many other examples in history has played an important role in making change happen."

In my own Christian tradition, Jesus offers as clear a vision of what we need to do to help creation, and help ourselves, as can be found in any sacred text. What Jesus teaches, mostly, is ethics. His fundamental concern is with moral values. What Jesus is passionate about is making moral choices that transcend the conventional rationale that "everyone's doing it, so I will, too." "You have heard that it was said, 'An eye for an eye and a tooth for a tooth,' " he says in the Gospel of Matthew. "But I say to you, do not resist one who is evil. But if any one strikes you on the right cheek, turn to him the other also; and if any one would sue you and take your coat, let him have your cloak as well; and if any one forces you to go one mile, go with him two miles. Give to him who begs from you, and do not refuse him who would borrow from you."

Moral choice, Jesus says repeatedly in a variety of contexts, calls us to a spiritual dimension that challenges our conventional way of doing things. Stretch beyond the conventional to help others, Jesus says. In Luke, he instructs his dinner host to invite the blind, the lame, and the poor to the dinner banquet. The poor, the hungry, and the oppressed, he tells us, are blessed.

Felecia Shelor, host for our Tuesday-evening gatherings, has taken the blessedness of the poor and oppressed to heart. For the past few years, she has traveled extensively in Israel, the West Bank, and Gaza, working with Israeli and Palestinian peace activists to promote justice for Palestinians, a Palestinian state, and a secure peace for all Israelis and Palestinians.

Jesus, she believes, has called her to do this vexatious, even dangerous, work. "Blessed are the peacemakers," Felecia believes fervently. As one well-informed Christian woman with many Israeli and Palestinian friends, she has demonstrated with time, effort, and her own money that some Americans still bear witness to the link between justice and peace in the Mideast.

"Jesus won't let me off the hook," she explains simply. "I have to do it."

Wisdom of this sort challenges us to help where help is difficult, to stretch beyond the comfort and conventionality of driving an SUV when SUV's gratuitously threaten our environment, to love and help—as Jesus tells us we should—our enemies. We are responsible, Jesus reminds us, not only for ourselves and those in our circle but for the divine gift of creation. When Jesus says, "Love thy neighbor as thyself," he means *neighbor* on a universal scale. We are endowed with a conscience that extends to all of life, and the choices we make are accountable to that conscience.

It's true that Jesus has nothing specific to say, in any modern sense, about an ethics of environmental responsibility. But he teaches that all choices make a difference, no matter how seemingly small. And no one is better at connecting the dots of those choices than Jesus.

Always, he insists upon congruence. As he says in Matthew, chapter 12, "Make a tree sound and its fruit will be sound. Make a tree rotten and its fruit will be rotten. For the tree can be told by its fruit. Brood of vipers, how can your speech be good when you are evil? For your words flow out of what fills your heart."

No punches are pulled here. Words and actions—for Jesus, there is no separation. We say we want to protect our disintegrating environment. Then why are we driving SUV's when something less wasteful and destructive will do? Actions and consequences—connect the dots. The SUV epidemic pollutes the air we breathe and ratchets up our dependence on oil. Pollute the air and we exacerbate global warming. Increase our dependence on oil and we remain wedded to oppression in the Mideast. Remain wedded to Mideast oppression that breeds terrorists and we become the target of those terrorists.

The dots always connect. One world. One ecosystem. If our personal choices make no sense for the one planet we all share, then that planet will no longer be a good home.

Rather than insulating us from how a large portion of the rest of the world lives, a simpler life reminds us that by consuming less and being better environmental stewards, we are better able to meet the needs of others. And a simpler life brings us closer to that congruence on which Jesus—in no uncertain terms—insists.

Simplicity alone may not be salvific. It may not alone heal the psychic fractures that many of us have, or completely nullify the un-Christian qualities of covetousness and self-aggrandizement. But I do think that when we make conscious choices to live more simply, we begin to be aware of what Walker Percy, in his marvelous novel *The Moviegoer*, calls "the search." We're lifted from a state of denial, that invisible despair that prevents us from being as helpful as we can be. "Despair," Kierkegaard says, "is precisely this: it is unaware of being despair."

Despair separates us from self-knowledge. It masks the fundamental reality that all true forms of love, and our ability to help others, are rooted in freedom—freedom, that is, from trivial or selfish desire, which is at the core of Buddhism as well as Christianity; freedom, as Jesus says in Matthew, "to say 'Yes' if you mean yes, 'No' if you mean no."

Congruence. Say what you mean and mean what you say. Know who you are and what you really need.

To help our world, then, is to help ourselves. We *are* the world—if there is one universal lesson from all the great spiritual teachers, that is it, plain and simple. *We are the world; the world is us.* That is the ultimate congruence. To help creation is to help ourselves.

"The purpose of life," the Dalai Lama once told students at Harvard Divinity School, "is to increase the warm heart. Think of other people. Serve other people. No cheating."

In soul work, perhaps the most important task we face is to examine our daily lives and ask ourselves these continuing questions: In what ways are we being helpful? And in what ways are we not? What specific things are we doing that help or injure creation and ourselves? And how can we better live our lives so that we can be more helpful?

The answers are often complex. They may change over time, and they will retain, in the aggregate, a dimension of mystery and uncertainty.

But the questions—"the search"—could not be more important. One soul is not too small to make a difference.

The Journey Continues

Spiritual growth has no end point. We grow by making an effort and by struggling, by staying open to new ideas and new experiences, by being better informed about ourselves, our world, and the consequences of our actions. But we do not "arrive."

As our physical universe expands, so can we. But there is no final ground, no absolute terra firma on which to stand. Though we often yearn for finality, for a fixed vision that explains all things, we cannot have it. As soon as we grasp it, certainty slips through our fingers like a wisp of smoke. Already, in our grasping, it is gone.

The tools I offer here for soul work come largely from my own experience. Try them, or some of them, if you can. But you will also find other tools. If there is one thing I hope this chapter has accomplished, it is that, in reading it, you will be reminded of your own spiritual resources and feel renewed in the hope of using them.

What is real differs from person to person, from generation to generation, from culture to culture—even from species to species. But we know that, for all their mystery and uncertainty, the universe we live in, the small planet where life has taken hold, and the endless caverns of the human psyche conjure a grandeur, a theater of infinite splendor and permutations.

Yet mortality whispers in our ear, like Death in Ingmar Bergman's indelible film, *The Seventh Seal.* "I have come for you," Death tells the weary knight, returning home to Sweden from the Crusades. Indeed he has, undeterred by the knight's bold attempt to elude him by winning a game of chess. After surviving savage battles as Crusaders, the knight and his squire have returned to a homeland besieged by plague.

My mother, Miriam, quoting her Methodist minister father, spoke often of "the brevity and uncertainty of human life." She was right, of course—mothers usually are. And what she meant was this: It's a big show out there, and inside ourselves. Pay attention while you still have the chance. You don't want to miss it.

Our souls journey onward. Day by day, we live our mundane lives, but as Thoreau tells us in *Walden,* our vision of the world and our place in it can expand forever. "Only that day dawns to which we are awake," Thoreau proclaims. "There is more day to dawn. The sun is but a morning star."